RELIGION on TRIAL

Cross-Examining Religious Truth Claims

REVISED EDITION

CRAIG A. PARTON

CONCORDIA PUBLISHING HOUSE • SAINT LOUIS

Published by Concordia Publishing House
3558 S. Jefferson Ave., St. Louis, MO 63118-3968
1-800-325-3040 • www.cph.org

Manufactured in the United States of America

1   2   3   4   5   6   7   8   9   10   27   26   25   24   23   22   21   20   19   18

Dedication

This book is dedicated to
Dr. John Warwick Montgomery: lawyer, theologian,
philosopher, and most important, friend.

In celebration of the Annual Study Session of the
International Academy of Apologetics and Human
Rights in Strasbourg, and the 10th anniversary of the
publication of your Tractatus Logico-Theologicus, which
teaches well that sapiens nihil affirmat quod non probat.

Contents

Foreword

The secular culture of the Western world is hostile toward Christian orthodoxy. As a consequence, Christians are rediscovering their rich history of defending the faith (or "apologetics," from the Greek *apologia*). The contemporary interest in apologetics has to a large extent brought about a revival of the philosophical defense of Christianity. This has resulted in a good-news and not-so-good-news situation. The good news is that important philosophical arguments from the patristic and medieval eras, such as those of Athanasius and Aquinas on God's existence, have been given new life for the contemporary scene. The less-than-good news is that these same philosophical arguments have a somewhat limited value. Convincing someone to become a theist is a necessary but not sufficient step in the apologetic process. The New Testament tells us that "even the demons believe" that God is one (James 2:19). Philosophical arguments do not have the ability to fully focus on the crux of the Christian position, namely the factual case for the death and resurrection of Jesus Christ. I once heard someone say, "Philosophy is very good at defining and describing the problem but not great at solutions!" If philosophical apologetics is not the most effective apologetic method, what can be used?

Fortunately, a small group of philosophers themselves have seen the weakness of their field and have recommended a way forward. One analytic philosopher said, "Logic is generalized jurisprudence . . . arguments can be compared with lawsuits."[1] What he meant was that for centuries, lawyers, judges, and juries have been dealing with the major issues that society faces. They resolve civil disputes and enforce criminal law on subjects by hearing relevant and admissible evidence in support of claims. Legal rhetoric and argumentation

---

1   Stephen Toulmin, *The Uses of Argument* (Cambridge: Cambridge University Press, 1986), 7.

based on the rules of evidence is absolutely essential in order for courts to reach sound conclusions. For centuries, the courts have been exercising and using practical reasoning based on evidence to discover the truth.

A small group of lawyers have taken their cue from analytic philosophers and developed a legal methodology in the area of apologetics. Legal apologetics is a branch of apologetics that says the historical evidence available in support of Christianity when viewed through the lens of common-law rules of evidence vindicates the truth of Christianity. Craig Parton is at the center of this apologetic school. The volume you hold in your hand is a legal brief for the contemporary seeker of religious truth. Parton describes the chaotic contemporary religious scene and acknowledges the challenges one faces in making a religious choice. He then gives the seeker tools on how to determine truth—how do we get at the facts? What is "evidence" in the religious world? In language the layman can understand, he explains how lawyers get at the facts and the truth.

Mr. Parton then moves to the documents that support and communicate the Christian claim, the first 4 books of the New Testament—Matthew, Mark, Luke, and John. In lawyerly-like fashion, he builds an argument for their historic validity and reliability. Throughout this work, he carefully builds his case and effectively cross-examines the opposing views until he reaches his conclusion. His approach is identical to that of the 19th-century Harvard law professor, Simon Greenleaf, who put it this way:

> All that Christianity asks of men on this subject is that they would be consistent with themselves; that they would treat its evidences as they treat the evidence of other things; and that they would try and judge its actors and witnesses as they deal with their fellow men, when testifying to human affairs and actions, in human tribunals. Let the witnesses be compared with themselves, with each other, and with surrounding facts and circumstances; and let their testimony

be sifted, as if it were given in a court of justice, on the side of the adverse party, the witness being subjected to a rigorous cross-examination.[2]

While contemporary authors like Craig Parton are leading the legal apologetics school, it is in many ways a revival of what Simon Greenleaf did in the 19th century and what Hugo Grotius, the Dutch lawyer and diplomat, did in the 17th century with his *The Truth of the Christian Religion*. This school is one that seeks to defend Christian truth claims by applying the rules of evidence, standards of proof, and legal argumentation that take one right to the central claim of Christianity—namely that "in Christ God was reconciling the world to Himself" (2 Corinthians 5:19).

This approach is not unlike what the apostles did. As we examine the New Testament writings, we see Dr. Luke documenting and compiling "a narrative of the things that have been accomplished among us . . . who from the beginning were eyewitnesses" (Luke 1:1–2). Peter in his Acts 2 sermon provides a legal brief for the timing of the Messiah, a summary of the facts of His ministry, death, and resurrection along with the Old-Testament-fulfilled prophecies. Similarly, Paul, who was legally trained, lays out the case for Christ in a forensic fashion to an inquiring audience in Acts 17.

I am delighted to endorse this work by Craig Parton. For several decades, Craig has taught apologetics and defended the facticity of Christian truth claims on university and college campuses and also as a lawyer in lectures and debates from Berkeley to Cornell. He speaks across North America and each summer at the prestigious International Academy of Apologetics and Human Rights in Strasbourg, France. As a skilled trial lawyer arguing for a verdict, Mr. Parton succinctly places before the reader the evidence that directs one to the cross of Christ as the only viable religious option in this pluralistic and secular age. May the seeker in reading this book come to see the

---

2   *The Testimony of the Evangelists* (Grand Rapids: Kregel Classics, 1995), 41.

Christ as described by John the apostle: "From His fullness we have all received, grace upon grace. For the law was given through Moses; grace and truth came through Jesus Christ" (John 1:16–17).

THE HONOURABLE DALLAS K. MILLER
Justice of the Court of Queen's Bench
Lethbridge, Alberta, Canada
On the Feast of the Epiphany
January 6, 2018

*"When one person
suffers from a delusion,
it is called insanity.
When many people
suffer from a delusion,
it is called Religion."*

—RICHARD DAWKINS[1]

*"We ... don't
believe in ghosts or
elves or the Easter
Bunny—or God."*

—DANIEL DENNETT,
DARWINIAN PHILOSOPHER[2]

---

1   Richard Dawkins, *The God Delusion* (London: Bantam Press, 2006), 28.

2   Daniel Dennett, "The Bright Stuff," *New York Times*, July 12, 2003, www.nytimes.com/2003/07/12/opinion/the-bright-stuff.html.

Religion: Ruin, Remedy, or Mere Relic?

Religions are worldviews. They claim to address the primary questions of our existence—where we came from, where we are going, and why we are going where we are going. Everyone is religious, because everyone has a worldview,[3] even if that worldview is that we came from a totally purposeless beginning and are returning to dust, and that this life is largely what novelist William Faulkner (echoing Shakespeare) called "sound and fury, signifying nothing." Thus, in one very important sense, everyone who has ever walked on this earth is thoroughly religious, from Mother Teresa to Madonna, from Stephen Hawking to Sigmund Freud, from Carl Jung to Karl Marx, from Buddha to the Beatles.

However, for good reason, the following perceptions exist: (1) religion is the true source of the problems in the world (one need only witness terrorists of all races and creeds who have strident and extremist religious views and the negative connotation that comes

---

3   Timothy Gill, well-known for promoting the right to same sex marriage across America, displays fervor and a level of tolerance often associated with religious zealots when he says, "We're going into the hardest states in the country. . . . We're going to punish the wicked!" ("Wicked Ways," quoted in *The Weekly Standard*, August 7, 2017, www.weeklystandard.com/wicked-ways/article/2009041).

with the word *fundamentalist*); (2) religion, unlike science, is hostile to intelligent factual inquiry[4] and involves, in the final analysis, issues of personal taste and mere matters of subjective preference ("You have faith, but I put my trust in the assured results of science," or "You meet a psycho-social need by means of religion, a need that I fulfill quite ably through assiduous commitment to my local pub"); or, at best, (3) all religions are saying approximately the same thing, so there is no ultimate difference, or significance, in the direction one chooses to travel on the "spiritual road."

This viewpoint reminds me of a comment I recently heard on my local university's campus: "I was raised Jewish, but I go to an ecumenical worship service on campus, and my mother is trying out Buddhism." We hear this kind of talk regularly, so it is no wonder that many of us dismiss religion as a kind of psycho-social, babbling blend of emotions, hang-ups, superstitions, prejudices, and paranoia. In addition, with 10,000 distinct religions in the world, and 2 being added to that number *every day*, it is clear that religious options are truly a dime a dozen.[5] Choosing a religion must be akin to choosing an ice cream you like. It's all a matter of preference and personal opinion. And while religion leads to enslavement by adherence to ritual and genuflecting to hierarchical authority, "spirituality" can be enjoyed on immediate and accessible terms that involve a wholly personal journey of freedom and self-discovery. Thus, being "spiritual" is fine. Being religious, however, is suspect.

After all, haven't the psychoanalyst Carl Jung and mythologist Joseph Campbell definitively shown us that many of the world's religions do, in fact, have common *ceremonies* (i.e., animal sacrifices are often employed cross-culturally in religious rituals; monasticism

---

4   The French atheistic philosopher Michel Onfray puts it this way: "Monotheism loathes intelligence. . . . God puts to death everything that stands up to him, beginning with reason, intelligence and the critical mind" (see John C. Lennox, *Gunning for God* [Oxford: Lion Books, 2011], 27). Or, as former Superman Christopher Reeve said, "When matters of public policy are debated, no religions should have a seat at the table" (quoted in "Reeve: Keep Religious Groups Out of Public Policy," The Associated Press, April 3, 2003).

5   James B. Twitchell, *Branded Nation: The Marketing of Megachurch, College, Inc., and Museum-world* (New York: Simon & Schuster, 2004), 48.

is found in both Christianity and in Eastern religions, as is the use of rosaries and pilgrimages; Mormons also engage in baptisms; etc.)? Thus, it is argued that no *final* significance can attach to the choice one makes regarding religious options since no religion can claim superiority based on unique practices.

Common *activities*, however, do not equal a common *cause* of those activities (this is subject to the logical fallacy of *post hoc, ergo propter hoc*, literally, "after this, therefore because of this."[6] In fact, the teachings of the world's religions themselves are radically different, and it is the teachings that give the religious practices their meaning and focus. Thus, Mormons and Muslims may both claim to follow the Ten Commandments, but they do so to merit salvation, heaven, and eternal life. Christianity, on the other hand, claims that we are unable to follow the Ten Commandments, that we cannot merit heaven by our works, and that a main purpose of the Ten Commandments is to remind fallen humanity of its *inability* to merit heaven.

So, what if all religions were, in the final analysis, fundamentally *incompatible* in regard to their teachings? Perhaps all could be false in their basic claims, but are *any* of them true? And why should one even bother to test religious claims for "truth" in any event? Isn't truth a culturally conditioned perspective and therefore a wholly relative concept? And isn't this "logic" a uniquely Western—and therefore modern—imposition on human thought? What criteria should one employ to determine the truth of contradictory religious claims? If one really could determine the truth or falsity of particular religious claims (or at least realize that some positions may make no such testable claims whatsoever), then one would at least be involved in weighing the evidence for and against those claims. Under these circumstances, could standards of proof from science, history, and law provide value in weighing the validity—or testability—of these obviously gigantic "cosmic" claims of the world's religions?

---

6   An example of the *post hoc, ergo propter hoc* fallacy is concluding that because all divorced couples were previously married, marriage is, therefore, the *cause* of divorce.

Originally, universities in the Western world were committed to what they called the *universitas*—or the universal nature—of truth. All knowledge was believed to be intertwined, and the division of the university into "schools" was simply a pragmatic effort to categorize knowledge. The accepted understanding, at least through the time of the Renaissance, Reformation, and really even through the 19th century, was that if something is established as a fact, it is a fact for those living in California or Caracas, Singapore or Syria. $E=MC^2$ in Hollywood, Harlem, or Hanoi. There is no Mormon math or Shintoist science. All of Western knowledge, and certainly the rise of modern science (starting around the end of the Middle Ages), is built on this presupposition about the nature of truth.[7]

This book is an effort to start at the beginning, with a serious look at whether the world's religions are really compatible—that is, whether all roads lead up the same mountain, and if not, whether *any* of them can withstand a closer examination using as our guide the evidentiary methods developed in law, history, and science. *If* any religions are left standing, they (or it) must have claims made not in a corner somehow immune from rigorous examination, but testable by all serious inquirers using methods that have been employed in other fields dealing with truth claims.

More fundamental, if God is there and is not silent, answers may possibly, though not necessarily, be expected to questions relating to the meaning of life (since, after all, we may determine that the evidence indicates God exists, but that He/She/It has apparently chosen to remain silent about any interest in or intentions for humanity and the world). An adequate foundation may perhaps be provided for real and defensible (i.e., transcendent and thus cross-cultural) ethics and for knowing if history is actually going somewhere discernible, but only if God has spoken in a way we can *understand*. Our highest artistic aspirations (that is, the sense that we are partaking of a gift

---

7   For a discussion of the importance of this worldview in the work of the 16th century scientists Nicolaus Copernicus, Tycho Brahe, and Johannes Kepler, see John Warwick Montgomery, *Cross and Crucible* (The Hague, Netherlands: Martinus Nijhoff, 1973), 1–22.

when in the presence of great art, music, and literature) may also, as J.R.R. Tolkien says, be verified or confirmed if God is there and is not silent.[8] If God has spoken, we would expect to hear clear words about man and his condition (not naive or ambiguous "do your best" moralistic platitudes, of which our culture is tragically full), and whether there really are answers to the fundamental problems of our existence, including the reality of evil and suffering and the apparent utter finality of death. We would hope to hear a direct explanation of how the existence of evil in the universe is compatible with an all-powerful and all-good Being. We would, in the very best of all worlds, want a God who cared about our condition. A straight flush would be a God who entered our situation, spoke clearly, and somehow presented a remedy for our seemingly deep infection and bent to do evil or, at a minimum, not fulfill even our own internal moral code.

The 18th-century encyclopedist Dr. Samuel Johnson once mused that "when a man knows he is to be hanged in a fortnight, it concentrates the mind wonderfully."[9] The French existentialists (Jean-Paul Sartre, Albert Camus, Samuel Beckett) echo the findings of the depth psychologists (Sigmund Freud, Carl Jung, Mortimer Adler) that our mortality is the fundamental and tragic predicament of our time. As the poet John Donne wrote in the 16th century, "You ask for whom the bell tolls, it tolls for thee." Funerals remind us that the implications of our worldview could not be more serious and important.[10]

Religious claims should be put to rigorous cross-examination of the type used regularly in my profession as a trial lawyer. Such

---

8   J.R.R. Tolkien, *On Fairy Stories: Essays Presented to Charles Williams* (London: Oxford University Press, 1947), 83–84. Tolkien makes it clear that high art is "received" while popular art and culture is "used" or "consumed" and that high art (e.g., Rembrandt, Shakespeare, and Bach) points to a higher and deeper reality.

9   Quoted by James Boswell, *The Life of Samuel Johnson* (New York: Doubleday & Co., 1946), 413.

10   For a discussion of how contemporary American society's values of entertainment and denial of sadness has resulted in removing the body from funerals and replacing it with the tortuous "celebration of life," see "Funerals from Hell: Where Have all the Graveyards Gone?," *Modern Reformation* 19 (Jan./Feb. 2010): 6–9.

claims should not be handled with kid gloves, because they claim to provide answers to the most significant questions relating to the meaning of life and death. Nothing less than eternity may be at stake, and it is simply not acceptable to allow religions to get away with vague assertions like "try us, you'll like us and your life will get better, your cholesterol will be lowered, you will have more flexibility and strength, and you will experience mindfulness, be in a safe spiritual place, and be at peace with the universe all while using your yogic global brain."

So, whether you are utterly convinced that you are one with God or the divine or that you are an insignificant piece of matter in a gigantic but ultimately purposeless cosmic game, or you are positive that God may be there but is deathly silent, or you are sure that your "religion" is true because it makes you feel good about your balanced spirituality and integrated personality, you should not fear a relentless search for the truth.[11] Such a quest is what this book intends to pursue.

---

11   Though Millennials now comprise the largest percentage of "religious nones," they now self-identify as the strongest contingent of the "spiritual but not religious" segment of the population, and more than 80% have a "deep sense of spirituality" and "wonder about the universe." See Ben Sasse, *The Vanishing American Adult* (New York: St. Martin's Press, 2017), 42.

"Every existing thing is born without reason, prolongs itself out of weakness and dies by chance."

—JEAN-PAUL SARTRE[1]

---

1   Jean-Paul Sartre, *Nausea*, trans. Lloyd Alexander (New York: New Directions Books, 1964), 180.

CHAPTER ONE

This Present Religious Chaos

The current religious buffet table offers a staggering variety of options. In my particular town of almost 100,000 people, there are more than 200 religions represented.[2]

All religions make various assertions about God, "The Ultimate," or the final purpose of existence. As we mentioned, the similarity of religious practices leads many to conclude that religions really teach the same core principles. However, often the reason people conclude this is more a function of reading the Quote of the Day on the local Unitarian Church's sign (where Buddha, Jesus, Muhammad, and Krishna get equal playing time on the marquee and end up supposedly saying the same thing about world peace and social issues) than it is a serious comparative analysis of what various religions *in fact* teach.

In short, people *want* religions to say the same thing, because they want to bring unity out of diversity so that it "will all work out in the end."[3] All will live happily ever after. We desperately, and

---

2   In reference to my town of Santa Barbara, a recent article on the city as a center of training of yogis from all over the world called the practice of yoga Santa Barbara's "shared lifestyle and our worldwide brand" that has "drawn mystics, healers, and mind-body enthusiasts" to its "Himalayas-by-the-Sea" geography for over a century. See "Yoga Teaching in Santa Barbara: A Mecca for Training Programs and Practice," *The Santa Barbara Independent*, August 24, 2017, 25.

3   "The desire for religious unity, though not logically justifiable, is eminently understandable"

understandably, wish this to be the case. Surely no one is *absolutely* wrong in any kind of final sense? Isn't each religious or philosophical position like the Indian parable about the various blind men who examined the same elephant? Each man described the creature with whom he had no prior contact solely and exclusively from his own limited and tactile perspective (the elephant is described variously as a snake, a rope, and a wall, depending on the blind man coming in sole contact with the trunk, the tail, or its mammoth sides). The resulting descriptions were true as far as they went but wholly inadequate without incorporating what the others discovered about the elephant too. We do our best, hoping that if there is a God, nothing more will be required than trying our hardest with the limitations each one of us operates with every day. In any event, God grades on the curve (with D+ being "passing"), and any other standard would seem to be grossly unfair. The approach of "merit" is what we experience in work, school, and play and is confirmed hourly. It is the practical foundation for salaries, grades, and scores. Getting what you deserve in this life seems to be pretty much the way the world operates.

But fundamentally, the fact of the incompatibility of the world's religions is a *logical* incompatibility, not a sociological incompatibility. This means that the issues where they are in contradiction are of fundamental importance. Any effort to gloss over these differences by focusing on similar *practices* (e.g., many religions have a liturgy or form of worship or meditation, a priestly class, and monastic vows in certain cases) is exceedingly dangerous and is a basic misunderstanding of the religions of the world in the first place. This can easily be seen in how religions vary widely on the basic subjects of God, man, evil, history, authority, ethics and morality, and the way of salvation.

(John Warwick Montgomery, *Tractatus Logico-Theologicus*, 4th ed. [Bonn, Germany: Science and Culture Publ., 2009], proposition 1.121). Montgomery's *Tractatus* (itself fashioned after a book by a similar title done by the greatest philosopher of the 20th century, Ludwig Wittgenstein) is the foundation for the present work.

God Is Viewed in Fundamentally Incompatible Ways in the World's Religions

God is viewed in fundamentally incompatible ways in the world's religions; that is, God is viewed as One, Many, He, She, It, Us, Father, Mother, all of the above, or none of the above.[4]

Religions claim knowledge about ultimate issues, including the existence of God. Thus, in Atheism, there is no God. In Agnosticism, nobody can know one way or the other whether there is a God, and thus skepticism is the only reasonable position. Polytheists (e.g., ancient Greece and Rome and many tribal religions) hold to the existence of many gods, while Pantheists see God and the world as essentially one (Eastern religions, meditation cults and health and wellness spiritualities line up right about here). Christian Theism says that God created the world, is superior to it yet separate from it, and that He did not create the evil in the world.

For Islam, Allah is God and Muhammad is His Prophet. Jesus Christ was only a prophet or messenger from God. The central Christian claim that in Jesus Christ you find God Almighty veiled in human flesh is considered blasphemy in Islam. God is not Trinitarian in nature in Islam (i.e., Father, Son, and Holy Spirit).[5]

Judaism agrees with Islam in the belief that God is one and not Triune in nature, and that Jesus is not God and did not rise from the dead to verify His claim to be God. Buddhism holds that there is no "God" out there apart from the created world, but that spiritual enlightenment comes from following the eight-fold path. In Hinduism and many eastern religions, God is co-terminus with both man and nature. For Mormonism, Adam was once a God and we too can become gods. God the Father is an exalted man (a man who has progressed to godhood) with a body of flesh and bones.[6]

---

4   For a comparison of basic worldviews, see James Sire, *The Universe Next Door: A Basic World-view Catalog*, 5th rev. ed. (Downers Grove, IL: InterVarsity Press, 2009).

5   See Koran 5:72–75, 5116.

6   *The Doctrine and Covenants of The Church of Jesus Christ of Latter-Day Saints* (Salt Lake City: The Church of Jesus Christ of Latter-Day Saints, 2013), 130:20–22.

In Eastern-inspired thinking, *you* are God. For Christianity, God is Triune in nature, Jesus is fully God and fully man and is the second member of the Trinity and died for the sins of the world.

Our fundamental point is that though all these assertions about God may be wrong, they logically cannot all be right.

Man Is Viewed in Fundamentally Incompatible Ways in the World's Religions

The world's religions view the human person in fundamentally incompatible ways.

For example, Christianity views man as a psychosomatic unity (from the Greek *psyche* [mind] and *soma* [body]), with a body destined for a resurrection at the end of the age when all flesh will be redeemed. Flesh, blood, and matter are considered good, created by God and taken on by Jesus Christ when He became Man. The Eastern religions view the body as an impediment to enlightenment and something to be cast off or somehow set aside (the material world is "Maya," or illusion), while the soul is to be united with The Ultimate. No distinction between good and evil exists. As *Siddhartha* says, "Everything that exists is good, death as well as life, sin as well as holiness, wisdom as well as folly."[7]

Many religions even view man as basically good and improving, or at least improvable. However, such religious optimism is necessarily disappointed anew each morning by the daily headlines. All religions, save for Christianity, see humans on a quest to reach up to God, always striving and working and in need of the best-tuned system to make this effort productive. It is summed up in the adage "If people knew better, they would do better," as if education is the missing ingredient. If this were the case, the leading universities would be the safest places in the world for a young woman at night. In my

---

7   Hermann Hesse, *Siddhartha*, trans. Hilda Rosner (New York: New Directions, 1951), 116.

hometown of Santa Barbara, one of the unsafest places for young women on Friday night is the elite college community of Isla Vista.[8]

Each religion provides a system for man to follow. Hold to the guidebook, and you arrive in heaven, nirvana, paradise, or inner peace. Fail to follow the rules, and the result is hell, isolation, unhappiness, lack of fulfillment, stress and distraction, or some similar fate. Your destiny is directly linked, in these religions, to your ability to consistently and thoroughly follow that particular system.[9]

Evil Is Viewed in Fundamentally Incompatible Ways in the World's Religions

Christian Science (which was a part of my direct experience for many years) and some Eastern viewpoints assert that evil is an illusion of the unenlightened mind. Buddhism teaches that evil (Karma) plagues man's steps from one reincarnation to the next, and that suffering and evil are merely a problem of "perception" that can be overcome by meditative techniques.[10] Taoism and Confucianism consider mankind basically good and not in need of redemption. Zoroastrianism holds that both good and evil, Ahura Mazda and Ahriman, have existed from the beginning.[11]

Christianity teaches that every person has violated the will of God in thought, word, and deed and can only be saved by God's grace as manifested in Jesus Christ's death on the cross.

---

8   See "Isla Vista's Culture of Sexual Assault," cover of *The Santa Barbara Independent* (February 15, 2018)—lead article is entitled "Glorifying Sex and Tolerating Assault in Isla Vista" by Samantha Bean, pp. 25–29.

9   The Oxford scholar C.S. Lewis has explained the significance of man reaching to God as opposed to God reaching to man by explaining the use in the biblical narrative of the Greek words *eros* and *agape*. See Lewis's *The Four Loves* (New York: Harcourt Brace, 1960).

10   For a contemporary effort to argue that all suffering is really a problem of perception rather than reality, see Robert Wright, *Why Buddhism Is True: The Science and Philosophy of Meditation and Enlightenment* (New York: Simon & Schuster, 2017).

11   As discussed on p. 98ff., atheism would appear not to have any logical basis to argue against the existence of God based on the existence of evil. In short, an absolute standard would seem to need to be postulated before one can argue for the existence of evil and no such absolute appears possible without postulating the existence of a fully transcendent and perfectly good being (i.e., God).

History Is Viewed in Fundamentally Incompatible Ways by the World's Religions

Both the ancient Greeks of the classical world as well as adherents of many Eastern religions view history as eternal and as involving a never-ending cycle. Hinduism and Buddhism are generally indifferent to the fate of individuals, let alone the world, since individual identity and the world are ultimately pure illusion (Maya). Thus these two particular religious positions also do not have a strong track record of interest in advocating individual human dignity and human rights or the relieving of human suffering (note, for example, the lack of Buddhist hospitals compared with the pervasiveness of Catholic and other Christian-related health-care institutions), especially since such suffering is linked with past lives and the karmic circle lying at the foundation of the Hindu caste system.[12]

Christianity sees history as linear, focusing on the past coming of Christ and His death for the sins of the world. Christianity also promises an end to the history of this world, culminating in the second return of Jesus Christ in judgment of both individuals and nations and the transformation of the heavens and the earth.

Authority Is Viewed in Fundamentally Incompatible Ways by the World's Religions

In Eastern religions, the New-Age faiths, many cults and mind-body religions and in the plethora of yoga-related philosophies, inner experience is the touchstone for all significant truth. Other religions have books they claim as absolutely authoritative. For Mormons, it is the Book of Mormon. For Islam, it is the Koran. Christian Scientists look to *Science and Health with Key to the Scriptures*, by Mary Baker Eddy. Judaism places authority in the Old Testament, while Christianity looks to both the Old and New Testaments.

---

12   J.N.D. Anderson, *The World's Religions* (Grand Rapids: Eerdmans, 1972), 99–135, esp. 109, 123–124.

These authorities cannot be harmonized unless one suspends the laws of logic, which include the basic law of noncontradiction (simply put, *A* does not equal *non-A*; for example, Sacramento, not San Francisco, is the capital of California) and the subject-object distinction (when you view an insect under a microscope, you are not viewing your own projection of an insect but an objective being separate and outside of you—this is the whole rational basis for inductive scientific exploration).

Ethics and Morality Are Viewed in Fundamentally Incompatible Ways by the World's Religions

While there is some overlap in the teachings of the major religions of the world,[13] this "agreement" is actually quite superficial. One often hears the argument that the religions of the world are all going up the same ethical Mount Everest because they all agree on a common core of ethical principles. This is actually *very* misleading and hardly the case. Politicians and members of the media, along with adherents to the various religions themselves, regularly reinforce this misconception by ignoring distinctions and logical contradictions between the world's religions and emphasizing that they all involve "faith."

First, disagreement exists on some of the most significant ethical and moral issues of our day. For example, a man may marry up to 4 wives in Islam, but the wife is chattel that can be divorced by the pronouncement of *talaq* (Arabic for "divorce") 3 times.[14] In Christianity, however, the man is to marry one woman and is to love her "as Christ loved the church" (Ephesians 5:25), for "there is no male and female, for you are all one in Christ Jesus" (Galatians 3:28). Second, the motivation for the "ethical" conduct differs wildly in the world's religions. For example, ethical good works are required for

---

13   See "Appendix: Illustrations of the Tao" in C.S. Lewis, *The Abolition of Man* (New York: Macmillan & Co., 1947), 95ff.

14   Koran 65.

salvation in Judaism and Mormonism, while Christianity rejects any use of ethics or morality as means to earn salvation.

Finally, Salvation Is Viewed in Fundamentally Incompatible Ways by the World's Religions

In all the world's religions save one, salvation is a constant climb upward. Salvation is ascension by means of obedience, enlightenment, or self-denial and discipline.

Islam offers salvation to those who obey Koranic law. Mormonism teaches that Jesus, instead of being the Crucified and Risen Savior of the world, was a polygamist who had children through multiple marriages, and that He was originally begotten through sexual intercourse between Mary and God the Father.[15] Christianity claims that through God becoming man in His Son, Jesus Christ, and by Christ's perfect life and atoning death on the cross, salvation has been made freely available to all mankind.

Some people claim that there are two religions other than Christianity that also teach a "salvation by grace." These two religions are the Sri Vaishnava sect of Tengalai Hinduism and the Japanese Buddhist sect of Pure Land (Jodo and Jodo Shinshu). However, this similarity is only apparent and does not withstand serious cross-examination.

In Sri Vaishnavism, "grace" is really an emotional and sensuous realization that is entirely individual and self-centered; whereas in Christianity, Christ "died for all, that those who live might no longer live for themselves" (2 Corinthians 5:15). In Jodo and Shinshu, man ascends toward the Pure Land as man and is absorbed into space and time.[16] In Christianity, the saving action is all from God to man. God descended to become a real man. He lived a perfect life

---

15   Brigham Young, *Journal of Discourses* (Liverpool: F. D. and S.W. Richards, 1854–1886), 1:50–51; 8:115.

16   For two excellent discussions of these religious positions, see John Warwick Montgomery, *Giant in Chains: China Today and Tomorrow* (Milton Keynes, England: Nelson Word Publishers, 1994), 129ff. ("seeming parallels to Christianity are only skin deep"); and Anderson, *The World's Religions*, 132ff.

in man's stead and died an atoning death for man on a cross. These claims concerning God and His entrance into human history are claims presented as verifiable by the resurrection of Jesus Christ in space-time history.

In Confucianism, man is capable of the ethical ideal without the aid of a Deity or God, and salvation is understood in terms of moral self-attainment. Confucianism is "hardly more than a pure secularism."[17] Man can save himself without the assistance of a supernatural being.

The way of salvation in Buddhism is through negation or separation from this world and the denial of all desires. Following Gautama Buddha of the 6th century B.C. who delayed his entrance into Nirvana after Enlightenment, followers should too refuse Nirvana until others are led into that state as well. Thus Buddha entered history to show compassion, but the saving ethical truths (that is, the four noble truths and the eightfold path of enlightenment) he provided are quite independent of history—they are even independent of the question of the historicity of Buddha himself. Buddhism can exist without the existence of Buddha!

In Judaism and Islam, the transcendent God cannot become man, and the idea of a unique Son of God is idolatrous. The way of salvation is through strict adherence to the Law as revealed either in the Old Testament (Judaism) or in the Koran (Islam).

For Christianity, Jesus Christ enters history to accomplish, by His death and resurrection, a salvation which is incomplete without His historical involvement. Salvation cannot be merited by rational contemplation, philosophical speculation, mystical union with God, or even by good works but is a gift given freely to all who believe in Jesus' death for sinners and is based on God's totally unmerited favor.

---

17   James Legge, "Confucius," *Encyclopaedia Britannica*, 11th ed. (New York: The Encyclopaedia Britannica Company, 1910–1911), 6:912. Legge also authored *The Life and Teachings of Confucius* (1867), *The Life and Teachings of Mencius* (1875), and *The Religions of China* (1881).

Conclusion: The World's Religions May *All* Be False—They Cannot *All* Be True

Efforts to claim that "all religions say the same thing," or that one ecumenical religion can be established based on common teachings, inevitably perverts the central—and diametrically opposed—teachings of the world's religions. Such efforts are hopelessly naive and ultimately reduce all religions to the lowest common denominator, for example, "Love your neighbor," or "Listen to the voice of the 'faith' community." With utterly no substance attached to such vague platitudes, these end up being pep talks about ethics and moral living and remain devoid of specific content. Love is a *motivation only*—it says nothing about specific actions. The world is not in need of more good advice concerning moral codes.

Much discussion in contemporary circles continues over the importance of multiculturalism, safe spaces, and inclusiveness. The suggestion, at least on the surface, is that tolerance is the ultimate virtue. *Tolerance* and *acceptance* are, unfortunately and incorrectly, considered synonymous terms. Often there is no recognition of the plain fact that not accepting people's moral behavior does not equate with denying them basic civil liberties or with advocating throwing them in jail or persecuting them. There is also the suggestion today that questions of the actual content and distinctions in religious positions only lead to acrimony, hatred, racism, and persecution. Actually, tolerance ends up being a platitude based on wholesale ignorance of essential differences in the world's religions. Real tolerance can only begin to proceed when the true differences in positions are fully explored.

Thus we see that the alleged compatibility of the world's religions is, at the root, a logical incompatibility. This incompatibility is based on the fundamental and contradictory character of the world's religions. They simply cannot all be true.

For example, Christianity teaches that "there is salvation in no one else, for there is no other name under heaven given among men by which we must be saved" (Acts 4:12). Jesus Christ went on to teach, "I am the way, and the truth, and the life. No one comes to the Father except through Me" (John 14:6).

We are thus faced with the fact that religions do not teach the same thing—or even approximately the same thing. We arrive here at a dilemma. To determine which religious position, if any, is true requires serious attention to the central question framed in the next chapter.

"Truth [is] the majority vote of that nation that [can] lick all others."

—SUPREME COURT JUSTICE
OLIVER WENDELL HOLMES[1]

---

1   "Natural Law," *Harvard Law Review* 32, no. 1 (1918): 40.

Getting to the Truth Question: Will the *Real* Religion Please Stand Up?

In large part, the answers given to the question "What is truth?" end up not being answers at all, because they always beg the question. Many claim that the answer to the question "What is truth?" is supplied by "common sense," or "intuition," or "authority." We shall see that all three of these sources of truth are wholly inadequate in themselves to provide answers to ultimate truth questions such as the existence of God and whether God has spoken in a way that can be understood, the value and meaning of human life, and where history is ultimately going.

We note initially that some modern thinkers have concluded that a strict and all-encompassing Darwinian naturalism or materialism (which assumes matter is all there is or ever has been) makes the pursuit of truth of doubtful value. They reason that all truth claims "are as much products of chance as are tectonic plates and mutated viruses" and that "the idea that one species of organism (i.e., man) is, unlike all the others, oriented not just toward its own increased prosperity but toward Truth, is . . . un-Darwinian."[2] In short, this argument asserts that if we are simply advanced amoebas that have survived by adaptation to the environment, then our brains are products of random evolutionary forces akin to Darwin's random variations in nature.[3] Under this approach, one quickly concludes that all the great formative ideas in Western culture are essentially evolutionary accidents. One of the prime advocates of this position was the late Stanford professor Richard Rorty, who saw Darwinian naturalism as the precursor and foundation for the movement known as "postmodernism." For Rorty, just as "a cosmic ray scrambles the atoms in a DNA molecule" to produce a mutation, so too the ideas of Aristotle or the Apostle Paul or Newton could be "the results of cosmic rays scrambling the fine structure of some crucial neurons in their respective brains."[4] Thus, the seminal ideas and insights of these individuals have the staying power they do not because they reflect an objective reality, says Rorty, but because they are useful in helping people organize their experience and gain ground in the struggle for existence.

Unfortunately, like Darwinian naturalism itself, Rorty's position is self-refuting. For if there is no objective truth and all is the product of random variation, then Rorty's insights are the mere conclusions of random variation that have no more, or less, validity than any other position. In short, if the ideas in our minds are not true but

---

2   Richard Rorty, "Untruth and Consequences," a review of *Killing Time* by Paul Feyerabend, *The New Republic* (July 31, 1995): 32–36.

3   Thomas Nagel, *Mind and Cosmos: Why the Materialist Neo-Darwinian Conception of Nature Is Almost Certainly False* (Oxford: Oxford University Press, 2012), 27. Nagel, hardly a religious believer, points out that reductionist Darwinism has yet to explain the origin of consciousness or the mind and that "[e]volutionary naturalism provides an account of our capacities that undermines their reliability, and in doing so undermines itself" (reprinted by permission of Oxford University Press, USA).

4   Richard Rorty, *Contingency, Irony, and Solidarity* (New York: Cambridge University Press, 1989), 17. Of course, such a view is inconsistent with any attempt to justify a transcultural ethic and thus we should be unsurprised that the secular Jewish philosopher David Berlinski writes that Rorty "had no criticism to offer Nazi Germany beyond a personal sense of revulsion" (*The Devil's Delusion: Atheism and its Scientific Pretensions* [New York: Random House, 2008], 40).

only useful, then this same principle also applies with equal rigor to the idea of Darwinian naturalism. Darwin himself recognized the self-refuting nature of his insight, saying it resulted in "horrid doubt"[5] about the objectivity of his conclusions.

In addition, modern science and the modern university are predicated on the foundation that truth is attainable. Law, medicine, science, and history are also all predicated on an implicit rejection of the hypothesis of randomness found in Darwinian materialism. In fact, a strict materialism based on random variation did not, and could not, produce the confidence to even go forward in any significant measure in science. In addition, a strict materialism spells the end of any defensible transcultural ethics or morality.

What, then, are the various manners in which people have attempted to discern truth? There have been several approaches offered.

First, common sense and intuition are often offered as touchstones to resolving questions of truth. But these two sources have been proven time and time again to be anything but trustworthy. "Common sense," for example, is appealed to by adherents of mutually incompatible religious positions and thus it is not "common" at all! Similarly, if intuition was a reliable source of truth for all people, then all people would hold the same religious convictions, because all would have a common and innate pool of intuition that was universally accessible. Since this is hardly the case, it can in no way be said that intuition or common sense resolve truth questions.

Second, "authority" is often presented as the answer to religious truth questions. While an authoritative and unambiguous word from God might solve a legion of problems, it also begs the question. Where is that authority to be found?

---

5   "With me, the horrid doubt always arises whether the convictions of man's mind, which has been developed from the mind of the lower animals, are of any value or at all trustworthy" (Charles Darwin, cited in *The Life and Letters of Charles Darwin*, ed., Francis Darwin, vol. 1 [New York: D. Appleton, 1898], 285). Compare Darwin's relative humility about his theory with the narrow fundamentalism of Richard Dawkins who preaches that "It is absolutely safe to say that if you meet somebody who claims not to believe in evolution, that person is ignorant, stupid or insane (or wicked, but I'd rather not consider that)" ("Put Your Money on Evolution," *The New York Times*, April 9, 1989, section 7, 35).

Merely making a claim to such authority does *not* establish it. Many Christians make this basic error when they make assertions such as "I believe it because the Bible says it and that settles it." This is invincible ignorance, and avoids the basic question of whether the authority is itself trustworthy. The fact that the authority claims to be from God is hardly sufficient. Many authorities make this claim and yet contain mutually and utterly contradictory statements (e.g., Mormon doctrine teaches that the Garden of Eden was originally located in Jackson County, Missouri, which does not appear to be what Moses had in mind when writing the early chapters of the Book of Genesis).[6]

Every religious position has a source of authority. For Roman Catholicism, that authority resides in what is called the "teaching Magisterium of the Church." Muslims posit authority in the Koran, Buddhists have an 8-fold path, Mormons have the Pearl of Great Price and the Book of Mormon, and Christian Scientists have Mary Baker Eddy and *Science and Health with Key to the Scriptures*. Christians have the Bible. The obviously incompatible claims of religious authorities suggest that many false prophets have gone out into the world and continue to do so to this day. The dilemma is this: Which ones are false? To answer that question requires the ability to screen or test claims of authority from the outside *and with a criterion which is itself not created by the source of authority you are investigating.*

Thus "common sense," "intuition," and "authority" totally beg the question. For how does one know if the voice they are listening to is the voice of God or the voice of a demon? In Nazi Germany many were convinced that the voice of God was in the National Socialist Party. Today members of White Supremacist Groups or the Alt-Right hear God when they march and burn crosses, while others "tune in" to God via drugs, radical terrorist groups, or experientially based theology. Some televangelists appear to get messages directly from God—those messages appear most regularly to involve the need of

---

6   Smith, *Doctrines of Salvation*, 20–21.

viewers to provide their credit card number to the operators on the studio phone lines.

"Religious Experience" Does Not Determine Truth

Many claim truth through subjective religious experience, espousing a "testimony" as an unchallengeable link to the truth. However, unfortunately, there are as many religious experiences and testimonies as there are religions. More important, to say that "religious experience" equates to "religious truth" is to commit what Oxford philosopher G.E. Moore called the "naturalistic" or "socio-logical" fallacy.[7] One commits this error by equating what "is" with what "ought to be." One sees this in many uses of statistics (e.g., 65% of unmarried couples engage in behavior "x," which says nothing whatsoever of the "truth," or rightness or wrongness of behavior "x").

Experience simply cannot be the source of truth. Thus, those who tell someone to "try Jesus, or Buddha, or Muhammad, or Krishna, or Crystals, or Yoga, or Scientology, because He/She/It works," are as misled as those who would have you "try this red pill or try explod-ing bombs inside cafes, it works for me." Polygamy may "work" on a variety of sociological levels, but this says nothing about the objective truth or falsity of the position. More disturbing is the fact that ultimate religious positions require a commitment of the whole personality to their teachings. If those teachings ultimately turn out to be false, the psychological—let alone physical—damage can be devastating. If you hold to a religion that claims that the ultimate act of commitment is suicide, any later ability to investigate and poten-tially invalidate that particular religion's truth claims is problematic. The stakes could not be higher to engage in that investigation *before* committing to the position.

---

7   G.E. Moore, *Principia Ethica* (Cambridge: Cambridge University Press, 1962), 8–11. For an analysis of 30 logical pitfalls that people consistently make in discussing religion, see A.J. Hoover, *Don't You Believe It!* (Chicago: Moody Press, 1982).

Multiple "Authorities" Do Not Determine Truth

Some try to avoid the problem of verifying the authority by postulating *many* sources of authority. This, however, begs the question: will the *real* authority please stand up?

Certain religious positions attempt to get around the problem of authority by postulating a variety of sources of authority, all equal in weight and value. For example, Roman Catholicism and Eastern Orthodoxy speak of "Scripture and Tradition" as coequal sources of authority, while Anglicanism refers to "Scripture, Reason, and Tradition" as fundamental. The problem, of course, occurs when the various sources of authority do not harmonize, or worse, when they flatly *contradict* one another. Proponents of multiple sources of authority claim such contradiction never occurs, but they are at best naive about that claim.

The Protestant Reformer Martin Luther pointed this out to his Roman Catholic opponents when he said that their "Tradition" (e.g., existence of purgatory, use of indulgences to purchase forgiveness, Mary as mediator between her Son and fallen mankind) contradicted the primary source material found in the biblical authors and that Papal Councils were often in error. Similarly, reason may contradict Scripture or Tradition (how God can exist in three persons and yet be one God, how can God possibly become man at a point in time since God is eternal and timeless). Under those circumstances, what is a person to do? Deceive oneself into thinking that no such contradiction actually exists? Often adherents of multiple sources of authority go to absurd lengths to try and harmonize the clearly contradictory positions in these sources of authority. Worse, yet, after they admit the contradiction they will then dismiss it with the comment that "it isn't a recognized Tradition or teaching of our church anyway." This reminds one of the Englishman who denied that England had ever lost a battle. When confronted with a clear example to the contrary, his answer was always the same: "Well, you don't consider *that* to be a battle, do you?"

Thus simply saying that you have many sources of authority in your religious position begs the question.

Sincere "Faith" Does Not Determine Truth

There are some who claim that "faith" somehow resolves all doubts and answers all questions of logical contradictions between religious positions. Unfortunately, this also begs the question.

Some advocates of various religious positions claim that the key to unlocking the contradictions between "authorities" is to simply ignore them and have "faith."[8] Faith, it is argued, is where one must begin and if one exercises faith, then the religious position in question will be validated. For example, some Christians claim that faith is where you begin in examining the Christian truth claims. Faith magically validates all of Christianity to the inquirer, regardless of any alleged contradictions, logical fallacies, or factual errors one raises in opposition. A variation of this argument is the claim that if one just accepted the claims of the Bible, it would all make sense later. But many religious positions that are logically incompatible tell inquirers that they must first drink their particular brand of Kool-Aid to see if it is really Kool-Aid rather than hemlock. Such mutually incompatible claims to self-authentication are recipes for trouble. Some are literally hocking a lethal Kool-Aid, as the followers of the 1970s cult leader Jim Jones discovered. Jones orchestrated the suicide and murder of over 900 members of his apocalyptic commune (called the "Peoples Temple") in Jonestown, Guyana in 1978 by having them ingest a mixture of Kool-Aid laced with cyanide

---

8   Or in the case of Mormonism, when confronted with the clearly factually inaccurate claims of the Book of Mormon, the response is that the Mormon knows his religion is true because of a "burning in the bosom." We also note that "faith" is not restricted to religious people. One can have ardent faith *in* scientific materialism at a level that can only be considered religious. An example is the following comment by Harvard biologist Richard Lewontin: "We take the side of science in *spite of* the patent absurdity of some of its constructs, *in spite of* its failure to fulfill many of its extravagant promises of health and life, *in spite of* the tolerance of the scientific community for unsubstantiated just-so stories, because we have a prior commitment, a commitment to materialism" ("Billions and Billions of Demons," *The New York Review of Books*, January 9, 1997, http://www.nybooks.com/articles/1997/01/09/billions-and-billions-of-demons. Copyright © 1997 by Richard C. Lewontin).

and valium. More than 300 victims were children or infants whose parents administered the lethal concoction before taking it themselves.

Unfortunately, this is wholly misguided advice. "Faith" is a relational term that necessarily involves an object of belief. Christianity does not advocate faith *in faith*. There is no magic in believing. Believing is, per se, neither good nor bad. What is critical is the *object* of the faith. I can passionately believe that the 4-year-old child in the pilot's seat of my 787 jet to Paris is going to get me safely to France. My "faith" is utterly misplaced though. Likewise, I can believe that a medicine bottle has Advil in it for my headache. However, if the bottle ends up containing arsenic, my faith will not keep me from an appointment with a mortician. Similarly, I may have grave doubts that the Supreme Court of the United States sits in Washington DC rather than in Spuds, Florida. In either case, neither my faith nor my doubts change the underlying facts.

"Faith" Is a Weasel Word

It seems like not a day passes without the media or politicians or pastors speaking about "people of faith," as if this is a special category of people who somehow contracted "faith" or took the "faith" pill. The specific content of the faith being spoken of is never discussed. Indeed, the content of any particular faith is utterly irrelevant in these discussions. "People of faith" have access to a cauldron of truths that the rest of society apparently lacks.

The number of faith options in the world is growing daily and is currently in excess of 10,000 religions, cults, sects, and isms. Some of these positions radically contradict one another and some are positively harmful (e.g., drug-using cults, terrorist religions that advocate violence to achieve religious objectives, free-sex/communal religions usually involving a Guru of some type, Eastern healing and meditative philosophies that eschew all traditional medicine, vegetarian cultic sects advocating the ingesting of rare mushrooms, etc.). Even if you try only one of these harmful religious positions, there is utterly no assurance that you will be in any decent psychological or physical shape whatsoever once you are done experimenting with that position. For example, Nobel Prize winner Arthur Koestler experimented with both Communism and Eastern religion.[9] Each experiment left Koestler and his wife apparently even less able to discern the facticity of competing religious positions and resulted in total despair. Koestler and his wife ultimately committed mutual suicide.

How then do we go about investigating religious truth claims? That is the next topic of our discussion.

---

9   This resulted in his writing two books: *The God that Failed* (New York: Books for Libraries, 1949) and *The Lotus and the Robot* (New York: Macmillan, 1961).

CHAPTER THREE

"When you have eliminated the impossible, whatever remains, however improbable, must be the truth."

—SHERLOCK HOLMES[1]

1   Sir Arthur Conan Doyle, "The Sign of Four," in *The Complete Sherlock Holmes* (New York: Barnes & Noble, 1992), 111.

Sherlock Holmes Meets the Dalai Lama: How to Investigate a Religious Claim

Logic Anyone?

Logic and the empirical (or scientific or legal-historical) method are the only means by which a factually based religious position can be verified.

We have seen that religious positions of the "try it, you will like it" variety make no factual claims that could be falsified in principle. But by what method can the competing claims of authority be weighed and either dismissed or verified? It is our position that logic and the empirical method are the *only* appropriate methods to determine the facticity or falsity of competing religious claims.

But is not "logic" itself a Western concept? Actually, no. The word "*logic*" has no plural form. There are no "Zen" or "Southern Baptist" or "Norwegian" logics. Simply put, you cannot function in the world without employing logic. This is true regardless of whether you are in Shanghai or Santa Barbara, Delhi or Detroit. Without logic you would not know if you were talking to a human being or to an avocado. In the same way, without logic there would be no way of discerning if you were hearing the voice of God or the voice of Frank Sinatra. To reject logic is to reject the possibility of gaining knowledge or pursuing systematic education.

The most basic principle of logic is called the "law of noncontradiction"—meaning that something cannot both exist and not exist at the same time. This is why religions and cultures that supposedly reject and ignore "logic" as a weapon of Western imperialism will still send their future rulers to be educated in universities where the law of noncontradiction is honored in practice if not in theory since classes are still taught and degrees still awarded with the idea in mind that objective knowledge is possible. The title *"Professor"* implies one professes knowledge of some sort. In fact, the concept of the university stems directly from the foundation of Western European Christianity and its acceptance of the fundamental idea that the world stands separate from God and can be investigated through the use of the rational faculties, and that the investigation of that world and the relieving of suffering in that world are vigorously encouraged. Intelligibility ends up being the foundational presupposition of modern science—the idea that the world is knowable and organized.[2]

The law of noncontradiction teaches very clearly that Christianity's presentation of who Jesus Christ is (God Almighty in the flesh come to save sinful humanity by His death on the cross and His subsequent

---

2   For a fuller treatment of this idea, see John R. Polkinghorne, *Traffic in Truth: Exchanges between Science and Theology* (Minneapolis: Fortress Press, 2002), 30ff. Polkinghorne is past President of Queens' College, Cambridge; Fellow of the Royal Academy; and former professor of mathematical physics at Cambridge. See also Nagel, *Mind and Cosmos*, 16, who says, "In the natural sciences as they have developed since the seventeenth century, the assumption of intelligibility has led to extraordinary discoveries. . . . Without the assumption of an intelligible underlying order, which long antedates the scientific revolution, those discoveries could not have been made" (reprinted by permission of Oxford University Press, USA). For how recent discoveries in synthetic biology are more thoroughly explained by the presumption of an underlying intelligibility, see also Fazale Rana, *Creating Life in the Lab* (Grand Rapids: Baker Books, 2011).

resurrection three days later) and Islam's presentation of Jesus Christ (a mere enlightened man and a prophet of God, but definitely not God in the flesh and definitely not the savior of the world) cannot both be right. They may both be in error, but they cannot both be equally true.

Of course, no one need be logical or live according to logic. You cannot be arrested for being illogical. People who insist on rejecting logic are given a padded room and medication all the while they attempt to eat the silverware and argue that Donald Trump is the reincarnation of St. Francis of Assisi. One can reject logic, but if one does so they eliminate the ability to communicate with others and eliminate the ability to discover truth. In my state of California, those who deny logic seem to make particularly large incomes as "personal spiritual guidance trainers" for Hollywood celebrities.

In addition, the denier of logic will necessarily be employing logic and the empirical method almost every moment of every day. Why? Because the real world still exists, and one will still be run over whether in the streets of Pittsburgh, Paris, or Pyongyang if the empirical method is not employed of looking both ways, weighing the evidence, and making a decision to cross the street. This occurs regardless of whether one is a Rastafarian or a Buddhist or an Islamic fundamentalist or a Yogi or a Christian believer.

Thus, *everybody* uses logic out of sheer necessity. But logic itself does not tell us the "stuff," or facts, of the world. It only shows us how to interrelate facts. The use of logic does not commit a person to *any* particular religious position. It is simply required to get anywhere in investigating the world. Therefore logic, in and of itself, does not compel one to accept that Allah is God and Muhammad is His prophet, nor does it compel the belief that Jesus Christ suffered under Pontius Pilate, died, and rose again from the dead.

While logic tells us how to interrelate facts, the empirical method tells us how to determine the facts of the world. The empirical method is used every day in the courts of law. It is the basis for all legitimate scientific endeavors and historical investigation. All that law courts do in a jury trial is provide a forum for the "re-creation of history." Trial lawyers present to juries a version of what happened in the past. Many legal trials can involve cases where the central facts of the case may have occurred a half century earlier. I had a trial recently where the issue was how to interpret the founding documents of a company in business for over a century. The empirical method is used by lawyers every day to investigate those facts. Juries use a version of that method to determine what the facts of the case happen to be, so that the relevant law can be applied to those facts.

How Holmes Would Examine the Claims of the Dalai Lama[3]—Applying the "Empirical Method" to Religious Claims

Sherlock Holmes laid out the conceptual framework for investigating religious truth claims:

> If we wish to arbitrate metaphysical and religious claims . . . the *sine qua non* is to appreciate the unyielding nature of the factual world about us. We do not create it by our philosophical speculations or religious ecstasies: it meets us at every turn, insisting that our ultimate claims conform to it. . . . It is not self-evident that I can discover facts, but I cannot change them.[4]

The empirical method operates as follows: First, one must determine the problem to be solved or the question to be answered (let's take,

---

3   For the definitive refutation of the popular (but wholly unsupportable) notion that Holmes moved toward Buddhism through contact with the Dalai Lama during the so-called Great Hiatus after going over the Reichenbach Falls with Professor Moriarty, see John Warwick Montgomery, *The Transcendent Holmes* (Ashcroft, British Columbia: Calabash Press, 2000), 87–95, addressing "Holmes in Tibet." One cannot conceive of two more opposite sensibilities: Holmes, for whom logic, evidence, and the aggressive confronting of evil were primary values, and Buddhism that "is not concerned with right and wrong . . . [and] is extremely flexible in adapting itself to almost any philosophy or moral teaching. . . .[and] may be found wedded to anarchism or fascism, communism or democracy, atheism or idealism" (Koestler, *The Lotus and the Robot*, 270–271).

4   Montgomery, *The Transcendent Holmes*, 126, citing Holmes, "The Problem of Thor Bridge," in *The Complete Sherlock Holmes*, 1056.

for example, whether Jesus Christ rose from the dead). Next, one formulates an answer or hypothesis that seems to explain the problem or provide an answer (for example, in the case of Christianity, the claim that God raised Jesus from the dead vs. alternative explanations such as the disciples stole the body, or later editors created a resurrection myth, or Jesus "swooned" on the cross and later resuscitated in the tomb and escaped). One next determines how to investigate the problem to be solved and what reliable data to employ in that investigation (e.g., review all eyewitness or primary source accounts vs. relying on the speculative comments of later writers about what might have happened, competent archaeological data, etc.). One then collects and records the data and rechecks and analyzes whether the hypothesis remains tenable or whether an entirely new or amended hypothesis is necessary in light of the factual data developed.

There are some who oppose using the empirical method to prove—or disprove—ultimate religious claims because they assert that this makes a method (i.e., the empirical or scientific-legal method) superior to God and thus it is idolatrous. These people argue that one should *assume* the truth of a religious position and then argue that the position is internally consistent. However, the problem with such an approach is immediately evident. Every religion says it is true, and many are at least internally consistent! The question is how to determine which religious position is in fact true. Internal logical consistency of a religious position is no basis for the acceptance of that position. Both Islam and Mormonism are logically consistent if one first accepts their fundamental starting points (for Islam that starting point is complete submission to Allah as God and Muhammad as his prophet, while for Mormonism it is a strict polytheism). Euclid's geometry is internally consistent but no one would argue that it is, therefore, the Word of the Lord.

Thus we by no means make an idol of a method by using the empirical or scientific-legal analysis to determine the accuracy of a religious position. The empirical method is simply a road map that we follow to see if we can arrive at the King's Castle and not at the local garbage dump.[5] Just because we use a map to get to the castle does not mean that once we arrive we fall down at the feet of the map and not at the feet of the Sovereign.

With Holmes as a guide, we will analyze religious claims by first asking whether the particular religious claim at issue even makes a factual claim in the first place. Such a claim, to be truly factual in nature, must be capable of being investigated by means of the empirical method and must be capable of verification or falsification. Unfortunately, 99.9% of all religious claims are not factual in nature and cannot be verified or falsified, even in principle.

Are Not All Interpretations Equally Valid Anyway?

But before we analyze competing religious claims, what if all interpretations in the end are equally valid? Haven't we then just wasted a tremendous amount of effort trying to get at questions of "truth" and "fact" only to discover that the interpretive grid we used to analyze those facts was wholly subjective? That brings us to our next very important point.

It is commonly suggested that facts are subject to a variety of mutually valid interpretations. However, this is contrary to the realities of science and law, both of which are disciplines where critical decisions effecting life, liberty, and property are made daily.

Facts are, in actuality, self-interpreting! Facts are themselves the final arbiters or judges of all competing interpretations. A proper interpretation of the facts should fit the facts just as a good shoe fits one's foot—not too narrow as to pinch (and exclude facts or data that are "inconvenient"), but not too loose as to let the foot slosh around (and thus be "consistent" with *any* view of the world).

Let's give two examples of what we mean. What of an interpretation of the Holocaust that argued that, as a matter of fact, Hitler loved the Jewish people and instituted the Holocaust in order to send them to heaven more quickly? Is that not a valid interpretation of the fact that

---

5   Montgomery, *Tractatus Logico-Theologicus*, proposition 2.385312.

Hitler exterminated 6 million Jews? Or consider the interpretation that Jesus was a Martian who deceived people into thinking that He was resurrected (as in Erich von Däniken's *Chariot of the Gods*) or that Jesus swooned on the cross and plotted with Joseph of Arimathea and Lazarus to revive in the tomb (as presented in Hugh Schonfield's *The Passover Plot*). Are not these valid interpretations of the facts?

We quickly see that no such interpretation can be maintained unless countless facts are discounted or totally ignored. *All interpretations are not equal.* The best interpretation is the one that fits the facts most completely.[6]

Indeed, the position of Postmodern literary criticism is that "no objective meaning" of any text is possible and all a person can do is tell "their story." Unfortunately, this position is an illustration of the logical fallacy known as "infinite regress"; that is, if no objectivity is possible, this applies to the person asserting this position also and the entire argument falls into solipsism or complete subjectivity.[7] The result is that no statement of any type carries *any* objective meaning: A statement is itself either objectively true (and thus refutes the position that no objectivity is possible), or it is a statement of subjective opinion and therefore is not verifiable.

The idea that "everyone has their own interpretation" is utterly rejected in fields where life and death are at stake. Radiation oncologists (cancer physicians), for example, do not live in the world of making up their own inner personal truths about how and where to attack cancer with highly defined and intense bursts of radiation.

---

6   UC Berkeley English Professor Frederick Crews' *tour de force* in this area is the hilarious book used by Crews as a college freshman textbook entitled *The Pooh Perplex* (New York: E.P. Dutton & Co., 1963). Here Crews writes each chapter himself under various pseudonyms, all the while claiming to give "deep" insights supporting the position that the Pooh story is better seen not for what all appearances it *is* (a children's book) but for its subtle attempts to present complex philosophical, psycho-analytical, and, yes, even theological positions. Thus, one chapter addresses Winnie-the-Pooh as "A Bourgeois Writer's Proletarian Fables," by "Martin Tempralis," with another entitled "A.A. Milne's Honey-Balloon-Pit-Gun-Tail-Bathtubcomplex," by "Karl Anschauung, M.D.," and even a chapter entitled in part "The Sacramental Meaning of *Winnie-the-Pooh*," by an Oxford theologian!

7   For a hilarious discussion of how the postmodern theorist Jacques Derrida complained bitterly and hypocritically that one of his opponents had treated him "unfairly" and had "misunderstood" Derrida's obviously clear (and objective?) position, see Millard J. Erickson, *Postmodernizing the Faith: Evangelical Responses to the Challenge of Postmodernism* (Grand Rapids: Baker Books, 1998), 156.

Similarly, courts regularly ask juries to arrive at one interpretation of the facts of the case and often send convicted defendants to their deaths based on that single correct interpretation. Serious scientists have now clearly recognized that if science is simply "politics and power plays masquerading around in a lab coat" rather than the pursuit of what in fact is true about the world, the future of that discipline is doomed.[8]

In addition, we must face the argument that objective truth is not possible because of the interlocking nature of the interpreter and the object of interpretation (the so-called Hermeneutic Circle). Proponents of this view then argue that all one can do is create values by their own decision (as urged by the existentialists) or "tell one's own story" (as say the postmodernists). We can agree that the observer brings to every investigation his own background and prejudices. However, it is a sign of maturity when one recognizes the world for what it is and distinguishes that factual reality from how one believes or desires the world to be.

One is reminded of the story by the humorist Robert Benchley, who described his disastrous semester-long effort in a college biology class. That class consisted of Benchley thinking he was diagramming an insect when he was instead meticulously drawing in his lab manual the image of his own eyelash as it fell across the microscopic field—evidence indeed of the danger of failing to distinguish between subject and object (and in Benchley's case, it was the obliterating of the line between what is being observed and the instrument used to observe it!).[9]

---

8   See the devastating critique of postmodernism's impact on science in Noretta Koertge, ed., *A House Built on Sand: Exposing Postmodern Myths about Science* (London: Oxford University Press, 1998).

9   Victor F. Lenzen, *Procedures of Empirical Science* (Chicago: University of Chicago Press, 1938), 28.

Religious Claims Are a Dime a Dozen

Religious claims do not equal religious *truth*. There is a multiplicity of religious "claims" floating around. Perhaps you have heard one of the following:

- "Brahman is All."

- "Jesus rose from the dead, but you can only confirm it is true if you first have faith."

- "I channel the timeless wisdom of the ancient Roman sage Maximus."

- "Muhammad caused the moon to come down and pass through his tunic. This occurred so quickly that no one noticed that the moon was missing."

- "God is Wholly Other and is Being Itself."

- "I believe God is in all of us."

- "The burning in my bosom confirms to me that Mormonism is true."

- "Jesus is in my heart."

- "Mindfulness brings inner peace and helps you reduce stress and experience oneness with nature and the universe."

All of these religious claims suffer from the same terminal malady—none of them can be *verified*. One might as well say that "God is 'The Great Vegan in the Sky' who gives me peace and purpose and forgives my sins." Verifiability is a critical component when dealing with religious claims.

Religious Claims Are Almost *Never* Verifiable

Once you realize that this is the case, you must stop asking "truth questions" about the religion. Why? Because you are making a category mistake and are involved in pure futility. The advocates of the religious assertions stated above will all appeal to the final arbiter of all religious claims—inner experience or the pragmatist's motto, "It changed my life."

Modern philosophy in the 20th century (especially the so-called "Vienna Circle" or the "Ordinary Language Philosophers" or the "Analytic Philosophers") spent considerable time analyzing the types of statements made in the area of religious or other ultimate claims. Statements were seen to fall into one of three categories:

- statements of logic or mathematics (called "analytic statements," from which this school of philosophy derived its name);

- statements of fact (referred to as "synthetic statements"); or

- statements of neither logic nor fact which were called "meaningless" statements (or "nonsensical").

A statement of logic or mathematics is a statement true by definition. But such statements really tell you nothing, said modern analytical philosophers, about the content or facts of the world. A statement of logic is something like 2 husbands + 2 husbands = 4 husbands. This statement is true if you know the definitions of the components. It tells you *nothing* about the factual nature of the world. One does not need to do an investigation of the world to determine the truth of this statement. A person could make the mathematical statement that "2 Cyclopes + 2 Cyclopes = 4 Cyclopes" and that is true regardless of whether Cyclopes exist. It is irrelevant whether Cyclopes exist or not. Logic, said the great 20th-century philosopher Wittgenstein, is the scaffolding of the world.[10] Logic provides structure and assists you in organizing the facts of the world, but logic does not help one whit in telling you the actual "stuff" or facts of the world.

---

10   Ludwig Wittgenstein, *Tractatus Logico-Philosophicus* (London: Routledge & Kegan Paul, 1961), propositions 1.1–1.21.

Conversely, a statement of fact or a synthetic statement is something that can be *verified* (via historical, legal, or scientific methods, for example). "Abraham Lincoln was assassinated in Ford's Theater," "Water is composed of 2 parts hydrogen and 1 part oxygen," and "Little green people live on Mars" are *all* statements of fact. While the last statement does not appear at first to be an assertion of fact, it is, at least in principle, verifiable—or at least falsifiable. With advancements in telescopes, radar, and technology, we could, with a reasonable degree of accuracy, determine if "little green people" actually live on Mars.

The last category is statements that are neither assertions of logic nor mathematics, nor are they factual in nature. Modern philosophers saw this last category as consisting of "meaningless statements." They are statements that may not be strictly or literally "meaningless," but they are statements neither true by definition nor true because they can be verified or falsified. While these "meaningless statements" may be meaningful to the person making them, and may reflect some mystical and nonverifiable religious experience, they are not subject to truth testing.

Now note how the statements with which we began this section are certainly *not* statements true by definition. That is, they are not assertions of logic or mathematics. Most important, though they may *seem* to make factual claims that can be verified or falsified, in reality, they do not. There is no way to verify or falsify any of the claims with which we began this section—no evidence can count for or against them.

Consider this statement of some Christian theologians: "Jesus rose from the dead, but it cannot be verified." Such a claim is actually *totally* meaningless. Why? If there is no way to verify the assertion that Jesus rose from the dead, exactly how does one come to believe its truth? If the response is "By faith," then why accept *this* particular claim by faith and not, for example, Muhammad's claim that he alone is the true prophet of God who brought God's final and complete revelation to mankind? To request someone to have faith in something which has no way of being checked out is to request pure credulity.

God the Father or God the Formula?

Similarly, a God of pure formality, logic, or mathematics that simply exists as a product of deductive reasoning would not be particularly helpful when you are on your back in a hospital room, having been informed you have three weeks to live. Such a formal God presumably would not be interested in a personal relationship with His/Her/Its creation. This kind of God could be carried around as a formula in one's back pocket, but there would simply be no assurance that such a god had the slightest interest in listening to and answering the prayers of its creation. Man presumably would benefit greatly from a God who cares, who listens, who has an interest in this world, and who is deeply personal and relational. If a god of pure logical or mathematical formality exists, we are not missing much by not connecting with "it."

But what if there was a God who was indeed personal? If He was interested in His creation it may not be irrational to conclude that He has given evidence of His existence and of His interest in His creation. And what if God had entered factual, gritty history in a deeply personal way? Again, it would not be irrational to conclude that He provided a means of verifying His entrance into human history. We would expect that there would be a way of verifying or falsifying the historical claim that God had entered human history. Are there rules that historians use to determine the likelihood of certain things having occurred in the past? Can those be employed to determine the "historicity" of a religion and its claims?

It is true that all religions are in some sense "historical" in that they arise in history. However, very few religions are dependent on the facticity and verifiability of their claims. Clearly the great so-called monotheistic religions (Christianity, Islam, and Judaism) make "historical" claims, as does Mormonism, in some sense. However, it appears that only one religious position—Christianity—pins its *entire* credibility on a particular historical event and even encourages rigorous examination and analysis of the facticity of that one event.

Christianity actually makes historically and legally verifiable claims that can be checked out in ordinary history by applying standard methods of historical investigation used all the time to determine the credibility of ancient and classical texts. The method we shall employ to investigate that central factual claim is the same method used all the time by courts and juries to determine questions of fact.

What Level of Certainty Can We Expect When Investigating a Religious Claim?

But what of the concern that historical questions can never be determined with *certainty*? Isn't it wise to be skeptical about history—especially *ancient* history?

First, complete historical skepticism as a position is illogical and self-refuting, since the present is always being transformed into the past. You create history all the time. What you were doing before you began reading this section of this book is now, technically speaking, "history." Second, a trial in a court of law is really a re-creation of history (i.e., what happened before the trial will be "re-created" at the trial). We live each day on the basis that the past can be accurately reconstructed and relied upon. Our society is built on the idea that history can be understood and "re-created" through the means of documents, photographs, testimony, artifacts, and so on. Third, matters of fact can *never* be 100% certain (i.e., there is always some level of uncertainty when investigating the empirical world, as our sense perceptions are not always reliable or accurate), but that does not prevent us from making decisions that are life and death in nature based on less than certain reasoning. Surgeons do this daily, weighing probabilities and making a decision based on historical records and their current evaluation. The fact that they are not 100% certain they are right in their diagnosis is not a reason to not go under their knife if the probabilities weigh heavily in favor of the diagnosis provided.

Thus, the central issue quickly becomes whether God has entered human history and whether sufficient evidence exists to verify that entrance into history. The skeptic surely stops us in our tracks here, does he not, since God entering human history would be a "miracle" and the assured results of science have disproved the existence of the supernatural and of the miraculous? In short, isn't it more rational to *always* go with a naturalistic interpretation of the evidence rather than a supernatural explanation?

As for the objection that miracles are not in principle possible (the argument of the 18th-century Scottish philosopher David Hume), the Einsteinian universe of relativity (all motion must be defined relative to a frame of reference so space and time are, therefore, relative and not absolute concepts) that we inhabit has told us repeatedly that it is more important to go with evidence over any Procrustean prior commitment to the impossibility of the miraculous entrance of God into human history.[11]

The reality of the situation is that miracles[12] cannot be ruled out without first checking the evidence. We simply do not know enough about the universe to dismiss factual claims *a priori* (or before checking out the evidence) without investigating those claims first to see if they hold water. Note that if a religious position makes claims that can be verified, those claims will be factual in nature. Thus they are claims that are capable of being verified *or* disproved. For example, a religion built on the claim that its leader is actually Abraham Lincoln risen from the dead is a verifiable religious claim. One could, for example, disprove it by exhuming the body of Mr. Lincoln which would disprove the claim immediately. But here we remember our fundamental argument: 99.9% of *all* religious claims are actually not capable of verification or falsification even in principle. Our response to such unverifiable claims should be: "Fine. But what distinguishes

---

11   As the Princeton mathematician David Berlinski says, Einstein's general theory of relativity in which old Newtonian forces vanished in favor of curved space and time meant the world was "far weirder" than ever imagined (*Infinite Ascent: A Short History of Mathematics* [New York: The Modern Library, 2005], 105).

12   For our purposes, a "miracle" can be defined simply as an event that is not adequately explained merely by reference to natural laws but points instead to transcendent power.

your claim from my claim that my beloved Australian Shepherd dog is actually God in the flesh risen from the dead and can forgive sins?"

We now see that *any* truly historical religious claim, even if evidence exists for it, will never reach 100% certainty. Issues of fact cannot in principle rise to 100% certainty. Only matters of deductive logic or mathematics can give one complete analytic certainty. But we have already seen that such strictly formal systems would not yield a personal God in any event, but likely only a God of a formula that can fit in my wallet by means of a 3 x 5 card or can be downloaded onto my smartphone.

So we are left with the reality of how the world works in matters of fact. History, law, and science are never completely 100% certain of their conclusions. They must always have some sense of humility and openness to being shown they are wrong and in need of correction if the facts turn out to be otherwise. Regardless of this, though, we continue to make life and death decisions based on probability reasoning and less than 100% evidence. Thus we condemn people to death by lethal injection and do life-threatening surgery based on weighing probabilities and coming to a decision based on less than 100% certainty of what the facts might be in a given court case or medical diagnosis. Every day in the courts of the United States people award millions of dollars to victims or litigants based on the weighing of evidence and probability reasoning. Therefore, when we come to historically based religious claims we should expect nothing different. Those claims, if they are truly factual, will always have some common denominators: (1) they will be verifiable or falsifiable, and will not consist of "hidden" knowledge that only spiritual people with "faith" can understand; (2) they will never attain 100% certainty; and (3) they stand as true whether people accept them as true or not.

We now turn our attention to finding whether *any* religious claims are truly factual claims.

CHAPTER FOUR

"Cross examination is the greatest legal engine ever invented for the discovery of the truth."

—JOHN H. WIGMORE[1]

---

1   *A Treatise on the System of Evidence in Trials at Common Law*, 3rd ed. (Boston: Little, Brown, and Co., 1940), Section 1367.

Religions on Trial

To this point we have seen that an enormously high percentage of religious truth claims may turn out, upon reflection, to be utterly unverifiable. Or looked at the other way, they provide no means of being falsified. The analytical school of philosophy in the 20th century concluded that all such nonverifiable or falsifiable claims (since they were neither statements of pure mathematics nor logic, nor were they "synthetic" statements of fact) were, in the final analysis, meaningless.[2]

We've seen how these Analytical Philosophers (who called themselves the "Vienna Circle") claimed that religious statements, since they were incapable of being verified or falsified, were technically meaningless. We have also seen that the canons of evidence as developed in historical research and particularly fine-tuned in the law have a core approach that can be useful to the determination of facts. Just as every legal case has factual underpinnings that must be determined, so religious truth claims—*if based on factual predicates*—should be verifiable or falsifiable. While neither the historical nor the legal method is capable of yielding 100% absolute results and both are probabilistic (i.e., both historians and juries can

---

2   For a fascinating, and short, debate by perhaps the two greatest philosophers of the 20th century (Wittgenstein and Popper) over "what can be known" about God and the world, see David Edmonds and John Eidinow, *Wittgenstein's Poker: The Story of a Ten-Minute Argument Between Two Great Philosophers* (New York: HarperCollins Books, 2001), esp. 142–164.

be wrong), to jettison this method of determining the validity of any particular claim is self-defeating. Why? Because society itself is held together by the assumption that facts are verifiable, that truth claims can be checked out and either verified or discredited (juries do this every day), and that matters of life and death are decided each day based on less than 100% certainty (doctors make diagnoses and take potentially life-threatening courses of action, juries send people to the executioner's chair, and people who fly in airplanes put their lives in the hands of sometimes unseen others all the time based on a weighing of evidence).

Our point is simple: We are entirely justified in employing a combination of historical and legal techniques to investigate primary religious claims. We have no other choice. For those myriad of religious positions which primarily consist only of offers of subjective "experience," "better life," "lower blood pressure," and "more peace" than other religions, we will not waste our time applying objective criteria to them since they involve no claims of fact. As previously noted, Nobel laureate Arthur Koestler's tragic effort to find truth by experience is a sober warning of the dangers of such an approach.

The Field of Verifiable, or Falsifiable, Religious Options Narrows the Field Considerably

There are three great "historical" religions—Christianity, Judaism and Islam. By "historical" we mean religious positions that would, at least on first glance, appear to pin their claims on certain events having occurred in history. Secondarily, Mormonism appears in part to also fall into this category. Every other religious position fails to give a factual, and therefore verifiable or falsifiable, basis for its claims. Neither Hinduism, Buddhism, Eastern-oriented faiths and meditative techniques, Shintoism, Taoism, mind-science faiths like Christian Science, nor sects like the Jehovah's Witnesses are wedded to history or fact to support their claims. These religious positions end up being "true" to the believer who enters in and "experiences" their truths or insights. Buddhism, for example, does not pin its truth or falsity on any historical claim of Buddha being true. In fact, Buddhism is technically not dependent on Buddha having even existed.

Or consider the Hindu claim that "Brahman is all." This claim is presented as beyond dispute, save for the slight problem of what it means! Does it mean that everything in fact *is* God? If so, then can we not assert with equal plausibility and sincerity that *nothing* is God too since the world contains a truly appalling amount of brutal and evil behavior in addition to acts of the highest levels of human kindness and compassion? If God is all encompassing and precisely coequal and One with evil and good, other than (as we shall see later) eliminating all bases for human rights activity, what exactly are we missing out on by not believing this fundamental principle of Hinduism?

In reality, however, neither Judaism nor Islam (let alone Mormonism) ends up making truly verifiable historical claims that can be seriously investigated.

For example, Judaism depends on the revelatory character of the Old Testament for its truth claims, and particularly on the truth of the Torah (first 5 books of the Old Testament). However, the earliest of all the complete Old Testament books (a Dead Sea Scroll of the Book of Isaiah) cannot be dated earlier than the first century B.C.[3] Therefore, the documentary evidence offers no primary or eyewitness historical attestation for the miraculous and allegedly revelatory events found in the Old Testament (though there is substantial archaeological evidence to support many of the historical references in the Old Testament).[4]

---

3   R.K. Harrison, B.K. Waltke, D. Guthrie, and G.D. Fee, *Biblical Criticism: Historical, Literary and Textual* (Grand Rapids: Zondervan, 1978), 31–32.

4   See, e.g., William F. Albright, *The Archaeology of Palestine* (Baltimore: Penguin Books, 1960); F.F. Bruce, *The New Testament Documents: Are They Reliable?* (Grand Rapids: Eerdmans, 1987); William Albright, *Recent Discoveries in Bible Lands* (New York: Funk & Wagnalls, 1955); Frederic G. Kenyon, *The Bible and Archaeology* (New York: Harper & Row, 1940); J. Barton Payne, *Encyclopedia of Biblical Prophecy: The Complete Guide to Scriptural Predictions and Their Fulfillment* (New York: Harper & Row, 1973); Nelson Glueck, *Rivers in the Desert: A History of the Negev* (Philadelphia: Jewish Publications Society of America, 1969), 31, where Glueck, the renowned Jewish archaeologist, says that "no archeological discovery has ever controverted a biblical reference"; and Alfred J.

Similarly, Islam claims that the Koran is God's final revelation to mankind. In support of this claim, we only have Muhammad's personal claim and utterly no verifiable evidence to back up that claim. To the contrary, the Koran (written in the 7th century A.D.) goes on to give supposedly definitive statements about what occurred in the first century with respect to the life and death of Jesus Christ[5] and then presents a personal morality of its founder that is (to put it charitably) utterly deplorable. For example, the Koran supports the inferiority of women, supports men having multiple wives even as young as 11 years old, supports enslaving opponents, supports the use of war and rape as methods of advancing religion, presents no basis for the protection of the human rights of the unbeliever, and supports the concept of jihad against infidels.[6] One example of the nonhistorical and analytically meaningless "miracles" of Muhammad given in the Koran is the story of the moon coming down and going in one sleeve of his tunic and out the other, then returning to the sky before anyone could notice it had left the sky.[7] No one else saw this event. How could one even in principle disprove this alleged miracle?

As for the Book of Mormon, essentially no competent scholar will attest to the work. In fact, Mormonism itself deflects any serious

---

Hoerth, *Archaeology and the Old Testament* (Grand Rapids: Baker Books, 2009).

5   Ibn Warraq, *Why I Am Not a Muslim* (New York: Prometheus Books, 1995), 148–149. Warraq notes here that there is good reason why no scholar ever cites the Koran as a historical source on the life of Jesus Christ: "No historian has ever looked at the Koran for historical enlightenment, for the simple reason that no historian will look at a document, which he will presume to be of human origin, written some six hundred years after the events it purports to describe when there are documents written some fifty or sixty years after the same events. We also know the source of the Koran stories, namely, heretical Gnostic gospels such as the Gospel of St. Thomas, which in turn have been dismissed as unhistorical."

6   Ergun Mehmet Caner and Emir Fethi Caner, *Unveiling Islam: An Insider's Look at Muslim Life and Beliefs* (Grand Rapids: Kregel Books, 2002). See also Koran 2:223, 282; 4:3, 11, 34. Allah gave Muhammad special permission to collect as many women as he wished (Koran 33:50). For an in-depth analysis of Muhammad's personal morality, see Robert Spencer, *Islam Unveiled: Disturbing Questions about the World's Fastest-Growing Faith* (San Francisco: Encounter Books, 2002), esp. 41–44. For the chilling but definitive account of how Islam treated the "People of the Book" (Jews and Christians) after conquering them pursuant to Jihad during the two main waves of Islamic expansion, see Bat Ye'or, *The Decline of Eastern Christianity Under Islam: From Jihad to Dhimmitude* (London: Associated University Presses, 1996). Ye'or concludes that Sharia does not permit Muslims to live peaceably with non-Muslims in the "one world" of theocratic Islam.

7   Koran 17.

historical investigation of the historical truth claims of Joseph Smith and the Book of Mormon. Joseph Smith's "witnesses" to the divine origin of the Book of Mormon hardly prove credible, and the assertion that the angel Moroni conveniently took the Golden Plates back into heaven leaves us with a totally untestable—or meaningless—claim.[8]

All of this is to say that by focusing our attention now on the truth claims of Christianity in particular, we in no way are showing religious or Western bias. Why? There are three very important reasons.

First, the consideration of a *claim* (in this case, the claims of Christianity) in no way predetermines its validity. Just as filing a lawsuit does not mean the claims in the lawsuit are legitimate or have factual support (as any experienced defense lawyer will attest), neither does investigating the claims of Christianity *presuppose* its truth or validity.

Second, if Christianity is found to be true, any religious affirmations contradicting its teachings must be rejected. So, by investigating Christianity we are in fact also treating the fundamental claims of other religions at the same time—to the extent those religions take positions diametrically opposed to Christianity.

Third, and most important, we can only investigate religious claims that actually allow for factual testing. We have seen that virtually all of the world's religions do not allow for such investigation because their claims are not factual in nature. It is pointless to spend time investigating the truth claims say of Buddhism or the New Age or meditative movements promoting vague notions of "mindfulness" when they make no such falsifiable claims.

Now, where do we begin in testing the truth claims of Christianity?

---

8   See F.E. Mayer's *The Religious Bodies of America* (St. Louis: Concordia Publishing House, 1961), 454–464, on the utterly unverifiable and, in most cases easily falsifiable, claims of Mormonism, including their claims about the origins of the American Indians; the setting up of the Temple of Zion in Missouri as the location of Jesus' earthly kingdom; Joseph Smith's tinkering with, and utter ignorance of, Egyptian hieroglyphics; and Smith's remarkable induction into the Priesthood of Aaron of Old Testament fame pursuant to a direct revelation to Smith from none other than John the Baptist.

Are the Foundational Documents of Christianity Sound? If Not, Do Not Proceed Further!

Since Christianity is a historical religion in that it claims, as we shall soon see, that certain events occurred in verifiable history, the soundness of these claims is directly linked to the soundness of the documents in which the claims are found. If the documents containing these claims are suspect and subject to corruption over time so that we really have little idea what took place originally, then all bets are off. Then even investigating certain pivotal claims in the documents (for example, whether Jesus died and rose again from the dead) is a completely fruitless task. If its foundational documents are unreliable (i.e., arise long after the events they record with only a trail of poor quality or conflicting manuscripts from which to re-create the original), then the claims and events recorded in those documents suffer a similar corruption and provide no basis for belief. Of course, one is perfectly free to choose an arbitrary religious position for the feelings or experience it gives or for other purely sociological reasons. If that is the approach, however, then precisely how does one choose what religion to begin with? Alphabetize them? Go with the one that promises the greatest reduction in stress during a lifetime? Start with the one where people seem happiest? Since some of the most bizarre cultists imaginable seem imminently happy (witness Jim Jones, David Koresh, L. Ron Hubbard of Scientology fame, and Mormon Polygamists featured on the hit cable TV show *Sister Wives* now in its twelfth season), this would not appear to be an adequate criterion. Psychiatric units have many utterly happy and confident and completely deluded occupants.

Certainly if the documents are sound and have come down to us in a reliable fashion, we can move to the next step of considering the facticity of the claims made in those documents. We are not saying at this point that just because a document has been successfully preserved through the ages (i.e., what we have is what the author or authors wrote), that necessarily means what they wrote is *true*!

However, the first step is to determine if the foundational documents (in this case, the material concerning the life and work of the founder of Christianity) have come down to us in a manner where we can say that what we read today is what was written originally. What we must *not* do is *presuppose* the soundness of the documents, for example by saying "I believe the Bible is the authoritative Word of God because it says it is." Instead, the standard method of historical and legal inquiry must be applied to determine whether the documents containing the essential claims of Christianity are reliable or not.

Isn't Pliny the Younger a More Reliable Source Than John the Evangelist?

But first, why not attempt to establish the truth or falsity of Christianity on the basis of "neutral" or secular writings of the time period, like Josephus, Pliny the Younger, Suetonius or Tacitus, since all have statements about Jesus Christ and the activities of the early Christian church? Would not such "secular" sources be more objective and less apt to embellish their writings with personal prejudice or bias?

The answer to why we do not take this strategic approach is simple: While references to Jesus by these secular historians make it virtually impossible to deny the historical existence of Jesus,[9] none of these references are in the nature of primary sources. That is, they do not derive from persons who themselves had contact with Jesus or his close associates. Judges in state and federal courts would say that these historians suffer from what the law calls a "lack of personal knowledge" about what they are testifying to and would be subject to a "hearsay" objection.[10] Why? Because they neither personally saw Jesus nor witnessed the events they recorded about Jesus' ministry or teachings. In addition, these so-called "extrabiblical" references are not contemporary with the life of Jesus and the events described.

---

9   For a definitive review of the 39 nonbiblical references that establish 110 facts concerning the life and ministry of Jesus Christ, see Gary Habermas, *The Historical Jesus: Ancient Evidence for the Life of Jesus* (Nashville: Thomas Nelson, 1984).

10   California Evidence Code section 1200; Federal Rule of Evidence sections 801 and 802.

The only primary source materials are the writings of four individuals (Matthew, Mark, Luke, and John) who claim at least to have had firsthand contact with Jesus and the events (as in the case of Matthew and John), or were close associates of the eyewitnesses and checked the data out for themselves (Mark and Luke). We, for now, totally ignore the fact that their writings are contained in a nicely bound set of writings called "the Gospels" or in a larger collection called "the New Testament" or "the Bible" (i.e., Old and New Testaments combined). The fact is that these four authors' accounts circulated *independently* and only later were included with other writings determined by the early church to be written by authors with firsthand contact with Jesus and the matters they were recording. Only those with such firsthand direct contact with Jesus (known as "apostles") were considered authors of authoritative and binding writings. This is also why the early Christians had no trouble excluding later books like the so-called "Gospels" of Thomas and Judas as wholly lacking authority or credibility, let alone the fact that they were not eyewitness accounts.

How Do You Establish the Reliability of Ancient Documents?

So our first inquiry is whether the writings themselves have come to us successfully or whether, as has been made wildly popular by Dan Brown's *The Da Vinci Code*, they were first collated, amended, edited, supplemented, and altered for generations by the Catholic Church (or perhaps by Emperor Constantine in the 4th century).

Note that we do not begin—as do many misguided Christians—with assuming the four authors of these primary sources give us "Gospel truth." In fact, we are not even calling these writings, or alleged biographies of Jesus, "Gospels." The term "*Gospels*" conjures up in the mind that these writers cannot be challenged by any serious inquirer and that we must assume for them a higher status at the front end of the investigation than is warranted. We start this inquiry only by applying generally accepted canons or methods of investigation to these four works that we would apply to *any* ancient or classical piece of literature in order to determine if it has come down to us generally in the manner in which it was composed.

So, it is critical to determine an answer to the question of how does one establish whether a document of classical Greek or Roman antiquity has come down to us today in a generally reliable form. In other words, how do we know that we have what was actually composed by the alleged author?

Fortunately, this question has been worked through very carefully and ably by a long line of scholars in other fields, particularly the fields of classics and ancient history. As fortunate, these scholars have no "religious" axe to grind by developing the standards they employ in their fields.[11] Note that the following tests presuppose absolutely *no* religious bias one way or the other. They are tests applicable to the writings of Plato, Homer, Catullus, and Suetonius, as much as to the writings of Matthew, Mark, Luke, and John.

These tests are commonly referred to in ancient historical scholarship as the bibliographical test, the internal evidence test, and the external evidence test. The *bibliographical* test seeks to determine how reliably the actual, physical document has come down to us today. The *internal evidence* test seeks to discover what the texts themselves reveal about their reliability. That is, do they even claim eyewitness status? And if the answer is yes, do the authors give evidence of the means, motive, and opportunity to present eyewitness evidence? The more removed the author is from the actual persons and events being written about, the more questionable the internal evidence will be and the more historically unreliable the resulting document. Finally, the *external evidence* test focuses on reliable materials and evidence outside the texts that either support or contradict the claims of the document itself.

---

11   Military historian Chauncey Sanders has summarized the tests we will apply in his work *An Introduction to Research in English Literary History* (New York: Macmillan & Co., 1952), 195ff.; see also Parton, *The Defense Never Rests: A Lawyer among the Theologians*, 2nd ed. (St. Louis: Concordia Publishing House, 2015), 99–118.

We will briefly apply these three tests to the authors whose works comprise the first four books of what came to be known as the "New Testament"—namely, Matthew, Mark, Luke, and John. Are they primary source documents that withstand the analysis brought by these three tests? Note that at this point we are simply trying to determine whether these four authors and their works are *reliable*, primary source documents. Nothing less. Nothing more. If they turn out to be unreliable and late sources, compiled by editors who wanted to feather their own nest egg or solidify the power, say, of the budding Catholic Church in order to suppress the masses and elevate their status, then we will have saved an enormous amount of time in not having to deal with Christianity as a valid factual "truth claim." These writings will have disqualified themselves from serious consideration since their religious claims will have been found to be contained in a totally spurious document, or in a document in which false information is so intertwined with the reliable material that it is impossible to separate the wheat from the chaff.

The Bibliographical Test Applied to Matthew, Mark, Luke, and John

Classical historians have trod the path we are on in their determination to establish the reliability of the textual tradition for the Greek and Latin works of the classical era. In general, we retain few, if any, original works of the Greek or Latin period. On a more contemporary note, we do not, for example, have even a single original manuscript of any of Shakespeare's 37 extant plays. As might be expected with ancient writings, the relentless crush of the elements over time (fire, wars, mishandling, damage due to age and storage) have left us with gaps between when the original work was composed and the date of the first copy.

It is, therefore, important to remember several points when dealing with ancient documents like Matthew, Mark, Luke, and John, whose authorship predates the invention of movable type. First, the *greater number* of copies that are in existence of any manuscript the more confidence one has that he can accurately replicate the content of the original document. For example, if one has only three copies of a document from which to construct the original, the confidence one has that the original can be reproduced is certainly much less than if one has thirty copies from which to conduct a comparison. Similarly, if one has three hundred copies of a document spanning hundreds of years and the copies show substantial agreement over a long period of time, one can have significant confidence that the content of the original document has likely not been corrupted.

In addition to the sheer number or quantity of documents, the *time gap* between the events recorded therein and the earliest copies becomes critical. The greater the time gap, the less confidence one has that the events recorded actually occurred as recorded. It will be instructive, therefore, to first inquire how works of classical Greek and Latin antiquity compare with the four authors of the life of Jesus Christ.

In general, the Greek and Latin classical works involve an exceedingly minute number of copies (no autographs exist in almost all cases), many of which first show up a millennia or more after the events that they record. Take the Latin poet Catullus as an example. Catullus wrote his poetic pieces from approximately 84–54 B.C. The earliest copies of his works date from the late 14th century and are known to us from only three manuscripts.[12]

Similar examples could be multiplied. Caesar's *Gallic Wars* (written from 58–50 B.C.) survive today on the basis of approximately ten manuscripts, the oldest of which is dated about 900 years after the events it records. Thucydides's (c. 460–400 B.C.) *History of the Peloponnesian War* is known to us through eight manuscripts, the earliest of which is dated about A.D. 900. However, F.F. Bruce, former Rylands Professor of Biblical Criticism and Exegesis at the University of Manchester, concluded that "no classical scholar would listen to

---

12   G. Lee, trans., *Catullus: The Complete Poems* (Oxford: Oxford University Press, 1989), ix–xiv.

an argument that the authenticity of Herodotus or Thucydides is in doubt because the earliest manuscripts of their works which are of any use to us are over 1,300 years later than the originals."[13] At the University of California in my hometown of Santa Barbara, one must read extensively in Catullus, for example, to obtain either a Master's or Ph.D. in Classics. There appears to be little concern that no original manuscripts of any of his work exists and that the earliest copies of Catullus date about 1,400 years after the poet lived.

The following chart[14] gives an overview of some of the best-attested works of antiquity, including when the original work was done, when the earliest copy comes to us, and the interval between the original and the earliest copy.

AUTHOR	DATE WRITTEN	EARLIEST COPY	TIME SPAN	COPIES
Caesar (Gallic Wars)	58–50 B.C.	A.D. 900	1,000 yrs.	10
Thucydides (Histories)	480–425 B.C.	A.D. 900	1,300 yrs.	8
Catullus (Poetics)	84–54 B.C.	A.D. 1400	1,500 yrs.	3
Plato (Tetralogies)	427–347 B.C.	A.D. 900	1,300 yrs.	7
Tacitus (Annals)	A.D. 98–117	A.D. 1100	1,000 yrs.	10
Pliny the Younger (Letters)	A.D. 61–113	A.D. 850	800 yrs.	7
Suetonius (The Twelve Caesars)	A.D. 75–160	A.D. 950	800 yrs.	8
Homer (Iliad)	8th century B.C.	400 B.C.	450 yrs.	643
Matthew, Mark, Luke, and John	A.D. 50–90	A.D. 200 (Bodmer Papyrus) A.D. 325 (Codex Vaticanus)	140–265 yrs.	15,000

13   Bruce, *The New Testament Documents*, 16–17.

14   The data used for this chart comes from the standard work on the topic by F.W. Hall, *A Companion to Classical Texts* (Oxford: Clarendon Press, 1913), 199ff., chapter entitled "Manuscript Authorities for the Text of the Chief Classical Writers."

What conclusion can we draw from this particular discussion? Much of what we know of the classical world is built upon the very thinnest of evidential or documentary trails. Two renowned classical scholars put it this way:

> When the great period of the revival was over (under the general reign of Charlemagne and his successors in the 9th to 11th centuries) some of the great works of Latin literature were still but a single manuscript on a single shelf. The slightest accident could still have robbed us of some of our most precious texts, of Catullus and Propertius, Petronius or Tacitus.[15]

Before turning our attention to how the biographers of the life of Jesus Christ measure up when compared to other works of antiquity, we should also quickly compare the manuscript authority for the Koran. Several differing versions of the Koran were circulating after the death of Muhammad in A.D. 632. A later Caliph (Uthman, the 3rd Caliph after the death of Muhammad) decided to collect all 24 disparate versions of the Koran save for one and proceeded to burn *all* the other copies. On the basis of this evidential trail, Muslim apologists claim that they have an uncorrupted and perfect single text from which all translations have come.

The only problem with this argument is that there is absolutely *no* evidence that the one version Uthman retained was the most accurate.[16] Thus when the followers of Islam claim they have no such problem with manuscript authorities because they have one pure text, the situation is actually quite to the contrary. Their "pure

---

15   L.D. Reynolds and N.G. Wilson, *Scribes and Scholars: A Guide to the Transmission of Greek and Latin Literature*, 2nd ed. (Oxford: Clarendon Press, 1974), 90. By permission of Oxford University Press.

16   See both Anderson, *The World's Religions*, 65, and Caner and Caner, *Unveiling Islam*, 86–87. We note here that even if the textual tradition is stable (i.e., it comes to us in a reliable form), we have seen that the text itself contains wholly unverifiable truth claims and directly contradicts the primary source material on the life and ministry of Jesus Christ.

and unadulterated text" allegedly dictated by Allah turns out to be totally illusory and easily capable of being falsified because of its bizarre and historically discredited statements about the life, death, and resurrection of Jesus Christ.

What is fascinating is that even though the time gaps are substantial between the date of the original composition and the earliest copy, the general authenticity and reliability of the great works of the classical world are simply not in doubt.

When we turn our attention to the writers of the four accounts of the life of Jesus Christ that are contained in the New Testament, the difference could not be greater. Even liberal and atheist biblical scholars agree that Matthew, Mark, Luke, and John are the best primary source recorders of the life of Jesus. For example, John Robinson, a liberal New Testament scholar, argues that all four of these works were written before A.D. 70.[17] William F. Albright, the Dean of American Archaeologists in the last century, concludes that "we can already say emphatically that there is no longer any solid basis for dating any book of the New Testament after about A.D. 80, two full generations before the date between 130 and 150 given by the more radical New Testament critics of today."[18] Albright also contends that "in my opinion, every book of the New Testament was written by a baptized Jew between the forties and eighties of the first century A.D. (very probably sometime between about A.D. 50 and 75)."[19]

Professor Bart Ehrman, a religious liberal himself, and chairman of the religious studies department at the University of North Carolina states it plainly: "The view of all serious historians of antiquity of every kind, from committed evangelical Christians to hardcore atheists" is that the "oldest and best sources we have for knowing about the life of Jesus" are the works of Matthew, Mark, Luke, and John.[20]

---

17 John A.T. Robinson, *Redating the New Testament* (London: SCM Press, 1976), 351–352.

18 Albright, *Recent Discoveries in Bible Lands*, 136.

19 Quoted by John Warwick Montgomery in *History, Law and Christianity* (Irvine: New Reformation Press, 2015), 17.

20 Bart D. Ehrman, *Truth and Fiction in The Da Vinci Code: A Historian Reveals What We Really Know about Jesus, Mary Magdalene, and Constantine* (Oxford: Oxford University Press, 2004), 102–103.

Let's see then just how these four writers match up under the bibliographical test when compared with other works produced during the same general time frame.

These works record events that took place primarily from A.D. 30–33. The earliest complete copy of all of the four works dates from around A.D. 325, a mere 300 years later. However, even this time gap can be substantially bridged by numerous partial copies, including portions dating from as early as the very beginning of the second century. We have a nearly complete copy of the books by John and Luke dating from the late second century. More impressively perhaps, the number of Greek manuscript copies alone of the New Testament (which obviously includes these works) is approximately 5,000. If Latin, Syriac, and Coptic copies of these four writers are included, the number swells to over 15,000.[21] In short, the brief time span between the original writings and the first copy, as well as the overwhelming number of copies of these writings, makes the evidentiary trail for all the other works of the classical or Latin world appear almost nonexistent. Yet the general reliability and integrity of the great works of antiquity are presumed and essentially beyond dispute.

Sir Frederic Kenyon, former Principal Librarian for the British Museum, put it this way:

> The interval, then, between the dates of original composition and the earliest extant evidence becomes so small as to be in fact negligible, and the last foundation for any doubt that the Scriptures have come down to us substantially as they were written has now been removed. Both the *authenticity* and the *general integrity* of the books of the New Testament may be regarded as finally established.[22]

---

21 Bruce Metzger, *The Text of the New Testament* (New York: Oxford University Press, 1968), 36ff.

22 Kenyon, *The Bible and Archaeology*, 288–289 (emphasis in the original).

John Warwick Montgomery, an English Barrister and American attorney, holder of 11 earned degrees and an authority on the evidence for the authenticity of Matthew, Mark, Luke, and John, puts it this way: "To express skepticism concerning the resultant text of the New Testament books . . . is to allow all of classical antiquity to slip into obscurity, for no documents of the ancient period are as well attested bibliographically as is the New Testament."[23]

But hasn't biblical critic Bart Ehrman shown decisively that the copies of the New Testament have more variants than words? Ehrman asserts, for example, that there are over 400,000 "variants" in the New Testament which is almost 4 times the number of actual words in the entire collection of New Testament writings! First, one would expect to find more variants in the literally thousands of copies of the books of Matthew, Mark, Luke, and John than in the 3 copies of Catullus. Second, and more important, Ehrman is being purposefully deceptive, as one New Testament grammarian has devastatingly explained:

> The Gospel of Mark consists of 11,260 Greek words. If a scribe introduced 25 variants into his copy of Mark, he would have averaged one mistake every 450 words. This, though, would still leave 99.8 percent of the Gospel uncorrupted. If subsequent scribes made 500 copies of Mark based on this "flawed" copy, and each one preserved all 25 mistakes, the total number of variants would now have risen to 12,500. This is more variants than words; but the variants are spread throughout 500 copies, while the text itself has still remained 99.8 percent intact. Ehrman knows this, but he continues to hype the quantity of variants as if this sounds the death knell for the reliability of Scripture.

---

23   John Warwick Montgomery, *Where Is History Going?* (Minneapolis: Bethany Publishing House, 1972), 46.

The real issue, however, is not the number of variants, but whether they are significant enough to alter our understanding of Jesus. In nearly every single case, discrepancies between copies are due to spelling mistakes, grammatical errors, different renderings of proper names, substituting proper names in place of pronouns, and changes in word order—none of which affect the text's meaning.[24]

In short, Ehrman's "more variants than words" claim is grossly misleading.

The Internal Evidence Test: Did Matthew, Mark, Luke, and John Possess the Means, Motive, and Opportunity to Record the Events Correctly?

While it is important to establish that a work has a trustworthy and reliable manuscript authority behind it, that is not the end of the inquiry. Even if copies come very early (even on top of the events they record), and even if there are a substantial number of copies that lead one to conclude that the original text can be accurately reconstructed, it is still quite possible that the work is generally unreliable. That can be the case if the "internal evidence" for the document is problematic. By this, we mean if evidence generated from within the document itself indicates that the authors were not in a position to have firsthand knowledge of the events they describe, or that they lacked the requisite skill or opportunity to get the facts right, or that they suffered from incurable bias, the document may still be unreliable in terms of providing a sound and verifiable base for its claims.

Fortunately this area of inquiry has been well-developed, particularly within the domain of the law, lawyers, and trial courts. Simon Greenleaf, the renowned professor of evidence at the Harvard Law

---

24   Mark Pierson, "The New Testament Gospels as Reliable History," in *Making the Case for Christianity: Responding to Modern Objections*, eds. Korey Maas and Adam Francisco (St. Louis: Concordia Publishing House, 2014), 53–54.

School in the 19th century and author of the definitive 3-volume treatise on evidence for its day, wrote widely on this precise topic. Greenleaf looked carefully at the question of whether the biographers of Jesus had the necessary means, motive, and opportunity to correctly record the events of the life of Jesus. The conclusion of Greenleaf, and numerous trial lawyers after him who have examined the evidence,[25] is that these writers more than meet the test. First, they had the means to do this kind of careful recordation. For example, Luke was a physician by training and he records that he set out to carefully develop the entire chronology of events of the life and ministry of Jesus. Luke provides enormous historical detail in his writings, which is precisely what one would *not* be doing if the goal is to deceive or play fast and loose with the facts. The following portion of the Book of Luke is the type of factual minutia we get from this author whose historical style has been compared to that of Roman historians Tacitus and Suetonius:

> In the fifteenth year of the reign of Tiberius Caesar, Pontius Pilate being governor of Judea, and Herod being tetrarch of Galilee, and his brother Philip tetrarch of the region of Ituraea and Trachonitis, and Lysanias tetrarch of Abilene, during the high priesthood of Annas and Caiaphas, the word of God came to John the son of Zechariah in the wilderness. (Luke 3:1–2)

One does not write this way in order to compose myth or fiction, or to try and cover up a conspiracy. Verification (or falsification) of

---

25   The list includes Hugo Grotius (the so-called "father of international law" in the 16th century), Sir Matthew Hale (Lord High Chancellor under Charles II in the 17th century), William Blackstone (codifier of the English common law in the 18th century), Simon Greenleaf (Dean of the Harvard Law School in the 19th century), Lord Hailsham (Former Lord High Chancellor in the 20th century), Jacques Ellul (former professor of law at the University of Bordeaux), Sir Norman Anderson (one of the great authorities on Muslim law in the English-speaking world), and John Warwick Montgomery (English Barrister and American attorney, author of over 60 books in six languages on the evidence for Christian faith, trial lawyer in some of the most important human rights cases of our day in the International Court of Human Rights in Strasbourg, France). For further discussion on the issue of why lawyers are so attracted to the Christian faith, see Parton, *The Defense Never Rests*, 85ff.

the author's accuracy is made so much more likely when potentially verifiable historical detail is used in this manner by Luke. If Luke was doing myth instead of history, or simply did not want to be checked out, he could have easily said "Some time ago, the word of God came to John the Baptist." One could not in principle refute that nonverifiable claim. In the law, liars inevitably talk in generalities so they cannot be pinned down, whereas credible witnesses often testify in great and graphic detail.

Manuscript authority F.F. Bruce, formerly of the University of Manchester, puts it well when he says any author who writes like Luke does here is "courting trouble, if he is not being truthful." His conclusion? Luke is a writer of "habitual accuracy."[26]

As for the other three biographers, Matthew was a tax collector and certainly not unfamiliar with the need to be exact and to provide sufficient detail to satisfy the skeptic. Mark is universally believed to have relied heavily on his direct contact with the apostle Peter and Peter's relationship with Jesus. Even with that said, Mark hardly portrays Peter as sinless or beyond moral reproach! As for the writer John, he was clearly an eyewitness to the life, death, and resurrection of Jesus, even to the point of being at the foot of the cross during the crucifixion itself. As he puts it, he recorded that "which we have heard, which we have seen with our eyes, which we looked upon and have touched with our hands" concerning Jesus and the events of his life (1 John 1:1).[27]

Even though the writers had the *means* or *ability* to do this important scribal work, they also had the *opportunity* since they were eyewitnesses. Clearly Matthew and John were within the original apostolic circle and directly witnessed the events they record (John says he saw the events "with his own eyes" while Matthew the Tax Assessor was present from the beginning of the ministry

---

26   Bruce, *The New Testament Documents*, 82, 90.

27   For a fascinating look at the way John uses legal principles of evidence in his Gospel and epistles, see Malaysian trial lawyer Henry Hock Guan Teh, *Principles of the Law of Evidence and Rationality Applied in the Johannine Christology* (Bonn, Germany: Science & Culture Publ., 2015), esp. 161–211.

of Jesus). Luke and Mark were close associates of this circle and their work indicates that they checked out the facts carefully and systematically (see, e.g., Luke 1:1–3). In addition, hostile witnesses abounded in those early days in which this material circulated. The equivalent of cross-examination in a courtroom existed as both the Roman authorities and the reigning Jewish religious leaders had every motive, means and opportunity to refute the early writings of the eyewitnesses. The lack of any primary source work whatsoever refuting these four accounts is important. In the laws of evidence, it is appropriate for a jury to presume that if a litigant has the means to marshal solid contradictory evidence at trial and fails to do so, the jury may conclude that no contradictory evidence exists.[28]

At this point one may wonder about the existence of the so-called Gnostic writings, such as the *Gospels* of Thomas and Judas, and other works popularized by Dan Brown's *The Da Vinci Code*. In point of fact, these second and third century (and later) works would never be admissible in a trial court as evidence concerning the life and ministry of Jesus as they are simply *not* primary sources. A hearsay objection to their admissibility would be sustained without question in any state or federal court operating in the common law world, and the authors of these works would never be permitted to utter a syllable of supposed eyewitness testimony about an historical figure that in fact actually lived centuries earlier than their account. These works lack *any* external confirmation of authorship or date, and thus there is no basis to conclude that they are primary source materials. In fact, the evidence is just the opposite. In the case of the Gospel of Judas, it was condemned as unreliable as soon as it began to be circulated.

---

28   California Evidence Code sections 412 and 413 ("Failure to explain or deny unfavorable evidence may suggest that the evidence is true." California Form of Jury Instruction, No. 205[1]). Clearly, the nascent Christian church could have been easily eliminated by the simple production of the body of Jesus if he in fact did not rise from the dead. The Romans and the Jewish religious leaders were both motivated and clearly powerful enough to produce that body under the circumstances (and the location of the tomb of Jesus was widely known since Jerusalem Supreme Court Justice Joseph of Arimathea volunteered to remove the body from the cross and place it in his family tomb—see Matthew 27:57–60; Mark 15:42–46; Luke 23:50–55; and John 19:38–42). The argument that Jesus' followers hid the body is legally uncompelling and absurd, for they then would have suffered death for what they *knew* was a lie.

Thus when these late and unattested works attribute acts or teachings to Jesus that at best cannot be confirmed in the eyewitness biographies of Matthew, Mark, Luke, and John, or at worst are directly contradicted by the primary sources, they lack historical value.[29] More important, when they contradict the eyewitness record, they must be *rejected*. This is basic legal-historical method and has nothing to do with religious bias or displaying favoritism to Christianity. Similarly, when the Koran, written 600 years after the life of Christ, contains material contradictory to the eyewitness accounts, it sows the seeds of its own destruction. No court would allow a witness like Muhammad, living 600 years after the events he writes about took place, to claim that he actually has the story right about the life, death, and resurrection of Jesus. This is why the Koran is simply *never* cited by any reputable historians as providing serious data concerning the life and teachings of Jesus Christ.[30]

But isn't it possible that these four writers produced cleverly devised forgeries? Perhaps in actuality the writings were pasted together hundreds of years later by politically motivated or power-hungry monks, or by scribes at the direction of Emperor Constantine, and made to look like they were firsthand accounts? Lord Hailsham, former High Chancellor of England, looked into this issue when investigating the case for Christianity. He concluded the following:

> [What] renders the argument invalid is a fact about fakes of all kinds which I learned myself in the course of a case I did in which there was in question the authenticity of a painting purporting to be by, and to be signed by, Modigliani. This painting, as the result of my *Advice on Evidence*, was shown to be a fake by X-ray evidence. But in the course of

---

29   For example, the Gospel of Judas claims that Jesus and Judas were close friends, that Jesus set up Judas to betray him, that they had a prearranged deal to do just that, and that Judas is actually a hero of the Church. The primary sources, however, do not portray Judas in this light, with Jesus himself saying of Judas that it would be better if he had never been born. See the Book of Matthew, for example, 26:24.

30   See the telling comment by Ibn Warraq in his work, *Why I Am Not a Muslim*, 148–149.

my researches I was supplied by my instructing solicitor with a considerable bibliography concerning the nature of fakes of all kinds and how to detect them. There was one point made by the author of one of these books which is of direct relevance to the point I am discussing. Although fakes can often be made which confuse or actually deceive contemporaries of the faker, the experts, or even the not-so-expert, of a later age can invariably detect them, whether fraudulent or not, because the faker cannot fail to include stylistic or other material not obvious to contemporaries because they are contemporaries, but which stand out a mile to later observers because they reflect the standards, or the materials, or the styles of a succeeding age to that of the author whose work is being faked.[31]

The consistent conclusion of legally trained trial lawyers over the last 300 years is that this material comes with the absolute best manuscript tradition possible, that it comes on top of the events that it records, that it is highly unlikely to have been forged, and that it contains the type of stylistic and factual detail you expect from truthful witnesses (i.e., liars love generalities while those telling the truth are not afraid of piling on the historical particulars).

The External Evidence Test: Does Reliable Extrabiblical Material Support or Contradict Matthew, Mark, Luke, and John?

The *external evidence* test focuses on reliable historical materials outside of the texts themselves that may assist in confirming or disconfirming what those texts say about themselves. Ancient secular texts rarely have such additional confirmatory information available since in essentially all cases, many centuries have passed between

---

31   Lord Hailsham, *The Door Wherein I Went* (London: Collins, 1975), 32–33.

the nonexistent original writing and the first copy.[32] In the case of the four biographers of Jesus, however, a wealth of such external information exists.

First, we have the testimony of direct followers of the writer John. These men—Papias of Hierapolis (ca. 70–155) and Polycarp of Smyrna (ca. 69–156)—record that John directly told them that the four books were indeed written by the traditional authors ascribed to them. Papias was told by John that Mark wrote the Gospel of Mark and recorded what Peter told him. Papias puts it this way:

> The Elder [i.e., John] used to say this also: Mark, having been the interpreter of Peter, wrote down accurately all that he [Peter] mentioned, whether sayings or doings of Christ; not, however, in order. . . . So then Mark made no mistake, writing down in this way some things as Peter mentioned them; for he paid attention to this one thing, not to omit anything that he had heard, nor to include any false statement among them.[33]

In a similar vein, Polycarp, also a disciple of the writer John, states that Matthew wrote the Gospel attributed to him, that Paul and Peter died under the Neronian persecution, that Mark wrote what Peter had handed down, and that Luke is the author, strangely enough, of the book attributed to him.[34]

Second, there is very strong support for the fact that Peter and Paul died under the Neronian persecution.[35] If this is the case, and their death likely occurred during that persecution around A.D. 64, then it is also reasonable to assume the Book of Acts in the

---

32   The scant external evidence supporting the works of central Greek and Latin writers such as Aeschylus, Thucydides, Cicero, Seneca, Euripides, Catullus, Petronius, Tacitus, Propertius, Vergil, and many others is covered in detail by Reynolds and Wilson in *Scribes and Scholars*, 186–213.

33   Eusebius, *The History of the Church*, trans. G.A. Williamson (London: Penguin Books, 1989), Book 3, section 39.

34   Irenaeus, *Adversus haereses*, 3.1.1.

35   Eusebius, *The History of the Church*, Book 2, section 25.

New Testament precedes that date. Why? Because the Book of Acts records the events of the lives of Peter and Paul in particular and would, most naturally, have recorded their deaths if they had died at the time the Book of Acts was written. Since their deaths are not recorded, it is most reasonable to assume that they were still alive at the time of the authorship of the Book of Acts. The importance of this for the early dating of Matthew, Mark, Luke, and John is this: If the Book of Acts predates A.D. 64, then Luke precedes that date also since the Book of Luke is widely considered to be a kind of "Part 1" to the Book of Acts. But Luke is not the earliest account of the life of Jesus. It is generally accepted that Mark and Matthew precede Luke. But remember, Jesus was crucified around A.D. 33.[36]

What we have, therefore, is the following chronology:

> A.D. 64—Terminus—death of Paul and Peter under Nero. Book of Acts written by then.
>
> Before Acts—Book of Luke is written.
>
> Before Luke is written—Books of Mark or Matthew are written.
>
> Jesus dies in approximately A.D. 33.

The time gap then between when these four works were first written and the date of the death of Jesus becomes so short as to be meaningless. This, in fact, is the conclusion of all the serious scholars cited already, including Frederic Kenyon, John Warwick Montgomery, and F.F. Bruce.

Third, the evidence from archaeology is simply compelling. In fact, archaeology has turned out to be the best friend that Matthew, Mark, Luke, and John ever had. Confirmation from the stones is

---

36   Amazingly, as noted previously, even the liberal biblical critic John A.T. Robinson dates all four of the first four books of the New Testament prior to the fall of Jerusalem in A.D. 70 and has Matthew or Mark as the first "biography" of Jesus to be completed. See Robinson, *Redating the New Testament*, 351–352.

overwhelming. For example, for decades critics of the four authors claimed that there was no historical evidence whatsoever that the Roman proconsul Pontius Pilate ever lived. There is now, however, clear verification of the existence of Pontius Pilate that was provided in the 1960s with the discovery of the so-called "Pilate Inscription," which is a first-century limestone tablet found in Caesarea with Pilate's name and the office he held ("Prefect of Judea") engraved upon it. This was the very first confirmation of the historicity of Pontius Pilate and his operation in Judea in the first century. This engraved stone can be viewed at the Israel Museum in Jerusalem.

There is also the harmonization of the previously thorny problem of the supposedly variant accounts of the date of the crucifixion found in the four books. The French Dead Sea Scrolls scholar Jaubert confirmed the existence of two calendars operating in first century Palestine (the sun-based Jubilee Calendar of Qumran and the lunar-based civil Roman Calendar), which solved a very difficult problem in church history of how to reconcile the apparently different date of the crucifixion as presented in the synoptic gospels (i.e., Matthew, Mark, and Luke) versus that set forth in the Book of John.[37] Finally, there is the discovery by the renowned archaeologist William Ramsay in the 1940s of the inscription of a Lysanias, tetrarch of Abilene, recited in the Book of Luke.[38] To that point it had been widely held that only *one* Lysanias had ever lived and that had been under the reign of Mark Anthony in the first century B.C. Yet the Book of Acts speaks of a Lysanias as tetrarch of Abilene during the time of Jesus. This recordation by Luke of the existence of a second Lysanias during the time of Jesus took a mere 1,900 plus years or so to be vindicated.

---

37   A. Jaubert, *La Date de la Cène. Calendrier biblique et liturgie chrétienne* (Paris: Gabalda, 1957). Jaubert's discovery is handled in great detail by John Warwick Montgomery in "The Fourth Gospel Yesterday and Today," *Concordia Theological Monthly* 34 (April 1963): 206ff.

38   Bruce, *The New Testament Documents*, 87–88; William Ramsay, *The Bearing of Recent Discovery on the Trustworthiness of the New Testament*, 1st ed. (London: Hodder & Stoughton, 1915), 297ff. This classic volume by Ramsay has been republished numerous times, even as recently as 2017 by Reink Books.

Thus the bibliographical, internal, and external evidence tests confirm the following: the books of Matthew, Mark, Luke, and John were composed by eyewitnesses on top of the events they record, that these works have a manuscript tradition that simply dwarfs any other works of antiquity, that they carry the evidence of internal consistency and personal attestation, and they are supported by the soundest of external evidence from archaeology. A.N. Sherwin-White, in his Sarum Lectures at Oxford on "Roman Society and Roman Law in the New Testament," sums it up well:

> It is astonishing that while Graeco-Roman historians have been growing in confidence, the twentieth-century study of the Gospel narratives, starting from no less promising material, has taken so gloomy a turn in the development of form criticism that the more advanced exponents of it apparently maintain—so far as an amateur can understand the matter— that the historical Christ is unknowable and the history of his mission cannot be written.

> This seems very curious when one compares the case for the best-known contemporary of Christ, who like Christ is a well-documented figure—Tiberius Caesar. The story of his reign is known from four sources, the *Annals* of Tacitus and the biography of Suetonius, written some eighty or ninety years later, the brief contemporary record of Valleius Paterculus, and the third-century history of Cassius Dio. These disagree amongst themselves in the wildest possible fashion, both in major matters of political action or motive and in specific details of minor events. Everyone would admit that Tacitus is the best of all the sources, and yet no serious modern historian would accept at face value the majority of the statements of Tacitus about the motives of Tiberius. But this does not

prevent the belief that the material of Tacitus can be used to write a history of Tiberius.[39]

Sherwin-White's point is clear: Such skepticism and hand-wringing seem to run rampant among critics of Matthew, Mark, Luke, and John when, at the same time, the documentary case for a well-known figure of the classical world, Tiberius Caesar, stands on a much thinner evidential reed and yet is universally accepted.

A Critical Cross-Examination of the Biblical Critics

Still, isn't it well-known that the Bible is a hodgepodge of diverse sources emanating out of a tortuously long oral tradition, often with multiple authors espousing conflicting theories within the individual books themselves, all with the goal of explaining mythological events that primitive Semitic peoples had no other ways of expressing? In short, has not modern scholarship (which is surely more scientific) shown the Bible to be untrustworthy?[40]

A well-known school of criticism arose in the 19th century that postulated that the first five books of the Old Testament were not written by Moses (as Jesus Christ believed and taught) but were a much later paste-up effort created from at least four distinct sources after generations of erratic oral tradition. This approach became known as the "JEDP Theory"—an acronym reflecting the first letter of each of the supposed four disparate sources for the first five books of the Old Testament.

This effort with respect to the New Testament is reflected in a novelistic fashion in Dan Brown's wildly popular work *The Da Vinci Code*, which presents the hypothesis that in the fourth century Emperor Constantine's underlings collated a variety of unreliable, non-eyewitness sources into the "New Testament" so as to present

---

39   A.N. Sherwin-White, *Roman Society and Roman Law in the New Testament* (Oxford: Clarendon Press, 1965), 187–188. By permission of Oxford University Press.

40   A modern biblical critic is someone who will "believe anything provided it's not in Holy Scripture" ("The Limits of Inclusiveness," *Newsweek*, November 10, 2003, 74).

Jesus Christ as a divine figure and to unify a Catholic Church that the Emperor could then more effectively manipulate.

This effort, unfortunately, has been found to be hopelessly subjective and unscholarly.[41] No less an eminent literary critic than Oxford Don and Cambridge University Professor C.S. Lewis says that this precise methodology (i.e., getting at the "true" sources of a particular work) was attempted with his Chronicles of Narnia series of children's fables. Lewis says the speculators engaged in quite "rational" and "reasonable" hypotheses as to the literary origins of Lewis' central figure in these novels, the lion Aslan. These "source critics" opined that Lewis likely got the critical images for Aslan from discussions with the legendary J.R.R. Tolkien, with whom Lewis met regularly to discuss their respective literary endeavors. These same source critics even analyzed the origins of Tolkien's mythological novel *The Lord of the Rings* and concluded that Tolkien's "ring" was clearly linked to the image of the mushroom cloud following the detonation of a nuclear device.

Interesting enough, Lewis concluded that the critics' conclusions were both "reasonable" and absolutely wrong. And not just wrong once but on *every single opinion* they offered on the "true sources" of Lewis' works.[42] The disturbing aspect of this discovery for Lewis was that the critics operating with his material were his contemporaries and were dealing with no foreign language or foreign culture. The so-called "source" or "form" critics of the biblical material, however, are speculating as to the true origins of material that is centuries old, written in essentially dead languages, and birthed in a culture totally foreign to that of 20th or 21st century England or Germany.

---

41   Author Anne Rice, creator of a fabulously popular series of vampire novels, and a recent convert to Christianity at the time, put it this way: "In sum, the whole case for the nondivine Jesus who stumbled into Jerusalem and somehow got crucified by nobody and had nothing to do with the founding of Christianity and would be horrified by it if he knew about it—that whole picture which had floated in the liberal circles I frequented as an atheist for thirty years—that case was not made. Not only was it not made, I discovered in this field some of the worst and most biased scholarship I'd ever read" (*Christ the Lord: Out of Egypt* [New York: Alfred A. Knopf, 2005], 313–314).

42   C.S. Lewis, *Christian Reflections* (Grand Rapids: Eerdmans, 1967), 152–166.

From a legal standpoint and from the standpoint of admissible evidence, there is a more profound problem with these efforts to get at the "true" sources of the biblical records: There are no such sources! The supposed sources that are speculated to have comprised the first five books of the Old Testament—called JEDP—*do not exist.*[43] You cannot go to a museum or a library or a university—or anywhere else—and ask to look at J, E, D, and P and compare them with Genesis, Exodus, Leviticus, Numbers, and Deuteronomy. The same situation exists for the supposed "true" sources that were collated and edited into what we now know as Matthew, Mark, Luke, and John. The application of this method of finding the "true sources" of the Gospels postulated a source called "Q." Author Q supposedly is the written material that one finds in Matthew and Luke but is not included in Mark. However, Q also does not exist as a document that can be handled and examined in a court of law—it is a product of pure speculation by biblical critics. As any competent trial lawyer will tell you, such testimony about a phantom written source would be subject to the "best evidence rule" (namely, the "best evidence" of "Q" is the "Q" document itself, not speculation about what "Q" might contain) as well as being objectionable as wholly speculative and inadmissible hearsay.

For example, this line of analysis was employed a hundred years ago to tap into the "real" sources and authors of works by the likes of Homer and others. The conclusion? According to H.J. Rose, recounting this bloody history in his standard *A Handbook of Greek Literature: From Homer to the Age of Lucian*: "The chief weapon of the separatists has always been literary criticism, and of this it is not too much to say that such niggling word-baiting, such microscopic hunting

---

43   Dr. Bruce Waltke, Ph.D. Harvard, and a former Fellow of the Hebrew University in Jerusalem, puts it this way: "Though one who has read only the popular literature advancing the conclusions of the literary analytical approach might not realize it, even the most ardent advocate of the theory must admit that we have as yet not a single scrap of tangible, external evidence for either the existence or the history of the sources J, E, D, P" (quoted in Albright, *The Archaeology of Palestine*, 2).

of minute inconsistencies and flaws in logic, has hardly been seen, outside of the Homeric field, since Rymar and John Dennis died."[44]

This effort has been wholly abandoned in the study of English ballads, the conclusion being that getting at the "true sources" and oral tradition of that material ends in hopeless speculation.[45] It is worth noting that the oral tradition from which such ballads supposedly evolved is in the realm of hundreds of years in length, while the most that can be said about any "oral history" of the New Testament material is that perhaps 20–30 years elapsed before the first written records appeared. Even that is actually quite extreme in light of the fact that the New Testament epistles, some of which predate the Gospels, have dates beginning at the latter half of the 40s of the first century and yet they even reference the fact that writings were *already* circulating at that time concerning the life and work of Jesus.[46]

Perhaps as telling, internal guerrilla warfare now rages among the "higher critics" of the biblical material as to the number and origin of the sources that underlie the biblical documents. For example, JEDP have now been supplemented by a "K" source (and sub-sources to "D"), and even now a K-1 source.[47] Critics of the book of Isaiah in the Old Testament have divided authorship into at least two distinct books instead of holding to the traditional understanding for centuries that, amazingly enough, Isaiah himself wrote the entire book of Isaiah. Why this effort to discredit Isaiah as the sole author? Because Isaiah contains predictions of events that occurred precisely as Isaiah predicted,[48] and since modern scholars simply know *a priori* that

44   H.J. Rose, *A Handbook of Greek Literature: From Homer to the Age of Lucian* (London: Methuen, 1934), 42–43.

45   John Drinkwater, *English Poetry: An Unfinished History* (London: Methuen & Co., 1938), 78.

46   A.H. McNeile, *An Introduction to the Study of the New Testament* (Oxford: Clarendon Press, 1953), 124; Bruce, *The New Testament Documents*, 14.

47   For a discussion of how Ugaritic studies were almost destroyed by efforts to employ this type of flawed methodology, see Cyrus Gordon's article "Higher Critics and Forbidden Fruit," *Christianity Today* 4 (November 23, 1959): 131–134.

48   The authority on Old Testament prophetic statements and their fulfillment is Dr. J. Barton Payne, who conclusively established over 100 specifically fulfilled prophecies in the Book of Isaiah

such predictions or prophesies cannot in fact occur save for some kind of after-the-fact fudging, the assumption is made that a second author—writing much later—must have created the prophetic material to fit events that had already occurred.

Lawyers, trained in the rules of evidence, would then expect that a discovery of very early manuscripts containing the Book of Isaiah among the Dead Sea Scrolls in the 1940s would reveal two authors (or, at a minimum, show a literary break between where one author ends and another begins). The scrolls show no such thing but instead provide evidence of a unified document.[49] Thus the oldest and best evidence we have on the authorship of the Book of Isaiah wholly refutes the contemporary critic's theory of multiple authors.

Is Not the Biblical Material Full of Errors and Contradictions?

We note initially that the area of alleged errors and contradictions in the Bible garners the award for more muddled thinking than perhaps any other topic of discussion. Often the simplest understanding of what an actual contradiction in fact *is* solves the problem (e.g., the claim that Matthew mentions only one angel at the tomb of Jesus while Luke mentions two—this is only a contradiction if Matthew stated that one and only one angel was present, which he does *not* say). A contradiction involves two assertions that cannot under any circumstances both be true.

For example, suppose you have admissible and reliable evidence that Mr. Schmatz was struck while walking in a crosswalk and died shortly thereafter. However, other witnesses unimpeachably testify that the same poor Schmatz was struck while riding in a van and died instantly. This is a clear and unexplainable contradiction, no doubt?

---

alone. See his *An Outline of Hebrew History* (Grand Rapids: Baker Books, 1954); *The Theology of the Older Testament* (Grand Rapids: Zondervan, 1962); and *Encyclopedia of Biblical Prophecy: The Complete Guide to Scriptural Predictions and Their Fulfillment* (New York: Harper & Row, 1973), esp. 278–320.

49   Gleason L. Archer, *Encyclopedia of Bible Difficulties* (Grand Rapids: Zondervan, 1982), 263–266.

But what if Schmatz was struck while crossing in the crosswalk and received fatal injuries at that moment? Schmatz was then transported by ambulance (a type of van) to a hospital to treat his surely fatal injuries. While being transported to the hospital in the ambulance, the luckless Schmatz's van-ambulance was crossing train tracks on the way to the hospital and was broadsided by a train, resulting in immediate death to Mr. Schmatz. Alas, all "contradictory" testimony is readily harmonized.

A plethora of scholarly works have analyzed in excruciating detail such alleged contradictions and have found sound grammatical and historical grounds for reasonable harmonization in every instance.[50]

One example of the problem is illustrative and has been briefly touched upon earlier. Since the time of the Enlightenment critics of the biblical material asserted that there is a blatant contradiction between Matthew, Mark, Luke, and John on the date of the crucifixion of Jesus Christ. The first three writers indicated that Jesus was crucified on the 14th day of the Jewish month of Nisan, whereas an analysis of John indicates that it was on the 15th day of Nisan. A clear contradiction, one might assume. But this problem was resolved in the middle part of the last century, when the French Dead Sea Scroll scholar Jaubert discovered the utilization of two calendars in Palestine during the first century.

Dorothy Sayers, one of the first women to be awarded a degree from Oxford and a renowned and skillful student of literature herself (particularly of Dante), looked carefully at the issue of alleged errors and contradictions in the biblical narrative and concluded as follows:

> [One] is often surprised to find how many apparent contra-
> dictions turn out not to be contradictory at all, but merely
> supplementary. Take, for example, the various accounts of the
> Resurrection appearances at the Sepulchre. The divergences

---

50   For an excellent example of this genre that goes back at least as far as Eusebius in the 3rd century and the correspondence between Augustine and Jerome in the 4th century, see Archer, *Encyclopedia of Bible Difficulties*, 263–266.

appear very great on first sight. . . . But the fact remains that *all* of them, without exception, can be made to fall into place in a single orderly and coherent narrative without the smallest contradiction or difficulty, and without any suppression, invention, or manipulation, beyond a trifling effort to *imagine* the natural behavior of a bunch of startled people running about in the dawnlight between Jerusalem and the Garden.[51]

The conclusion from this investigation is that Matthew, Mark, Luke, and John would stand up as admissible, nonhearsay evidence of the life of Jesus Christ in any court of law. Simon Greenleaf, former Dean of the Harvard Law School in the 19th century, put it well:

All that Christianity asks of men on this subject is that they would be consistent with themselves; that they would treat its evidences as they treat the evidence of other things; and that they would try and judge its actors and witnesses, as they deal with their fellow men, when testifying to human affairs and actions, in human tribunals.[52]

---

51   Dorothy L. Sayers, *The Man Born to Be King* (New York: Harper & Brothers, 1943), 19–20.

52   Greenleaf, *The Testimony of the Evangelists*, 41.

CHAPTER FIVE

"Make no mistake:
if He arose at all it
was as His body; if
the cells' dissolution
did not reverse, the
molecules reknit, the
amino acids rekindle,
the Church will fall."

—JOHN UPDIKE[1]

---

1   "Seven Stanzas at Easter" from *Telephone Poles and Other Poems* by John Updike, copyright © 1958, 1959, 1960, 1961, 1962, 1963 by John Updike. Used by permission of Alfred A. Knopf, an imprint of the Knopf Doubleday Publishing Group, a division of Penguin Random House LLC. All rights reserved.

How to Disprove Christianity

The fact that a document has been transmitted to us successfully, however, does not mean we are necessarily going to encounter testimony in that document that is of real value. Many historical works are "accurate" but trivial in the substance they transmit (one thinks of Einhard's biography of Charlemagne, which is a firsthand and nonhearsay account that gives us crucial information on such vital topics as the bathing habits of the first Holy Roman Emperor). What, in fact, do the New Testament materials present in terms of man's condition and the solution to that condition?

First, we note that many modern readers of the primary source material (Matthew, Mark, Luke, and John) give the impression that these works are hopelessly shrouded in mystery and obfuscation. They argue that only by unpeeling the onion of generations of encrusted oral tradition and mythology can the correct interpretation be divined, and probably then only by a religious studies professor. Nothing could be further from the truth. There is good reason why 5th graders easily comprehend this writing: the authors themselves are generally common folk with no interest in making their points difficult to discern.[2]

The Central Claim—God Closes In

To put it directly, the eyewitness record could not be clearer concerning the nature and character of the central figure in all four works, Jesus Christ. He claims to be nothing less than God Almighty in the flesh, come to earth to save sinful man by dying an atoning death on the cross for the sins of the world and rising again to verify his claims and vindicate the acceptance of that sacrifice before God the Father. Amazing? Quite. Unclear? Hardly.

Any thought that Jesus claimed to be merely a Buddha-type figure of peace and harmony was finally decimated in the 19th century by Albert Schweitzer. Schweitzer, in his groundbreaking work *The Quest of the Historical Jesus*, showed that there was no doubt Jesus considered Himself to be God Almighty come from heaven, the Judge of all mankind, and the One who would again return some day to judge the quick and the dead.[3] Schweitzer himself did not believe these claims of Jesus, but he concluded quite correctly that this is the only tenable view one can derive from an objective reading of the text. Statements such as the one found in John 8:24 are difficult to misinterpret: "I told you that you would die in your sins, for unless you believe that I am He you will die in your sins."

Oxford literary scholar and author of the Chronicles of Narnia, C.S. Lewis, put it nicely when he said that Jesus left the inquirer three options:

---

2   For a fascinating study of how one of Germany's leading biblical critics (a student of Rudolf Bultmann and Ernst Fuchs) had to literally learn the Bible again in a children's Sunday School class after disavowing her earlier higher critical views, see Eta Linnemann, *Historical Criticism of the Bible: Methodology or Ideology?* (Grand Rapids: Baker Books, 1990).

3   See also Albert Schweitzer, *The Psychiatric Study of Jesus* (Boston: Beacon Publishers, 1956), 11–15, where Schweitzer concludes that Jesus was psychologically stable even though he believed he was God in the flesh and yet was not! Past President of the American Psychiatric Association Winfred Overholser, who wrote the foreword for this work, states that Schweitzer's effort to find a Jesus who is sane yet wrongly thinks he is God is hardly successful.

I am trying here to prevent anyone saying the really foolish thing that people often say about Him: "I'm ready to accept Jesus as a great moral teacher, but I don't accept His claim to be God." That is the one thing we must not say. A man who was merely a man and said the sort of things Jesus said would not be a great moral teacher. He would either be a lunatic— on a level with the man who says he is a poached egg—or else he would be the Devil of Hell. . . . You can shut Him up for a fool, you can spit at Him and kill Him as a demon; or you can fall at His feet and call Him Lord and God. But let us not come with any patronising nonsense about His being a great human teacher. He has not left that open to us. He did not intend to.[4]

Claims to deity, however, are not uncommon. Psychiatric wards are crammed full of people with similarly deluded views of their own nature and ability. In the case of Jesus, though, the claims are tethered solely and completely to their ability to be verified by means of Jesus physically rising from the dead three days after the crucifixion. Leaving aside the psychiatric inquiry as to whether Jesus presents the profile of a deluded madman (especially in light of the fact that his teachings are considered the *sine qua non* of psychiatric health), would an actual and historical resurrection verify Jesus' claim to be God in the flesh?

As the depth psychologists and analytical psychologists have shown, death is the ultimate leveler of us all. The French existentialist philosophers (Sartre, Camus, Beckett) were clear that death is the final proof of man's total meaninglessness. Death, they said, refutes all efforts to find final meaning in the universe.[5] If, in fact, God ever became man, one would not be in the least surprised if the central

---

4   C.S. Lewis, *Mere Christianity* (New York: HarperCollins, 2001), 52. *Mere Christianity* by C.S. Lewis copyright © C.S. Lewis Pte. Ltd. 1942, 1943, 1944, 1952. Extract reprinted by permission.

5   See Albert Camus, *The Fall* (New York: Random House, 1956); Jean-Paul Sartre, *Nausea* (New York: New Directions Books, 1964); and Samuel Beckett, *Waiting for Godot* (New York: Grove Press, 1954), for the best articulations of existential man's total despair.

focus of that life and teaching was to give clarity and hope with respect to the horror of death. Jesus does exactly that in the New Testament record. Luke the historian says of Jesus that he "came to seek and to save the lost" (Luke 19:10). We would suggest that this is precisely the good news that the honest inquirer would hope he would hear from God if in fact God had ever entered human history to deal with our condition.

All this is to say that a resurrection from the dead has the *gravitas* or seriousness one would expect to vindicate a claim to deity. Clearly if Jesus attempted to ground his claim to be God in the miracle of healing hemorrhoids all over Palestine, the profundity of the event would not exactly go to the center of the human condition.

Jesus says his resurrection establishes his deity. Of course, he could be simply dead wrong about that interpretation (e.g., he could have resurrected but the correct interpretation of that is that we all resurrect anew each spring, like wildflowers). However, if he did accomplish his resurrection from the dead three days after his crucifixion, the law would easily find that he is the most qualified witness on the topic of the correct interpretation of that event. Particularly unsuitable interpreters of the meaning of that event are critics living centuries later who were not eyewitnesses of the event, whose worldview does not allow them to even consider the evidence for the resurrection, and who have certainly never accomplished *their* resurrection.

Don't Both Philosophy and Science Make the Resurrection Story the Stuff of Primitive Myth?

But we have gotten ahead of ourselves. Why? Because before we even consider the evidence for the resurrection of Jesus Christ, two seemingly devastating arguments have been raised against even the mere possibility of a resurrection. Those efforts have taken both a philosophical tack as well as a scientific line of argumentation.

There have been philosophical attempts to make even the investigation of the resurrection a meaningless task. We think in particular of the work of the 18th-century Scottish philosopher David Hume. Hume postulated (without any support, we might add) that there was uniform experience against the miraculous. However, Hume could only know that was the case if *all* reports about miracles were false. Yet, he could only know all reports about them were false if he assumed there was uniform experience against them. In fact, as C.S. Lewis and others have noted, Hume argued in a perfectly circular fashion.[6] Hume's fallacious argument allowed 18th-century rationalistic man—enamored as he already was with "natural laws" that supposedly totally and neatly explained the operations of the universe—to sit back in his easy chair and never investigate the factual case for the resurrection (i.e., the eyewitness accounts, details of the testimony as to the resurrection, the historical, legal, and medical evidence of the death of Jesus and his appearance three days later, etc.).

With respect to the so-called "scientific" argument against the possibility of a resurrection, the objection is anything but scientific. This position states that our current Einsteinian universe makes it unnecessary to check out supposed violations of natural law. The actual situation, however, is just the polar opposite. As Karl Popper and others point out, real scientists doing real science are anything but dogmatic, but recognize that their conclusions are based on the best data and subject to further refinement and change if the facts turn out to be otherwise.[7] Purely naturalistic theories have been shown to be much more the result of 18th-century man's religious commitment to rationalistic concepts of consistency and order, than a truly scientific effort to follow data wherever it may lead. No one

---

6   "I find it ironic that so many readers of Hume's essay have been subdued by its eloquence. And I find it astonishing how well posterity has treated [Hume's] 'Of Miracles,' given how completely the confection collapses under a little probing. No doubt this generous treatment stems in part from the natural assumption that someone of Hume's genius must have produced a powerful set of considerations. But I suspect that in more than a few cases it also involves the all too familiar phenomenon of endorsing an argument because the conclusion is liked" (John Earman, *Hume's Abject Failure: The Argument Against Miracles* [New York: Oxford University Press, 2000], 71; by permission of Oxford University Press, USA). For an excellent current analysis of the case for miracles, see Robert A. Larmer, *The Legitimacy of Miracle* (Lanham, MD: Rowman and Littlefield, 2017).

7   Karl Popper, *The Logic of Scientific Discovery* (Basic Books: New York, 1959); see esp. chapter 2, "On the Problem of a Theory of Scientific Method," 49–56.

has an ultimate pipeline to the center of the universe nor is anyone in a position to opine on what cosmic behavior is reasonable or not.

Whether a resurrection has occurred *since* the first century is also no argument against whether one *did* occur *during* the first century. Courts of law have no difficulty determining unique sets of facts that are not repeatable. The only question is whether the evidence is solid and sufficient to render a verdict that the event occurred, regardless of how "improbable" in light of our present knowledge of how cause and effect operate. As for the argument that first-century Palestinians were naive as to the nature of death and deeply gullible, there is simply no evidence for that position. In fact, the primary source documents give every indication that there was, as there is now, general recognition of the signs that declare a person is dead.

Who Moved the Stone?[8]

We have now come to the central question of the death and resurrection of Jesus. We have seen that the factual record containing the recitation of that event is in singularly magnificent literary shape. The eyewitness accounts had the benefit of circulating among hostile witnesses who had every means, motive, and opportunity to refute the claim. This means that the testimony circulated among an atmosphere effectively constituting what we know today as "cross-examination." The written record of contemporaneous refutation of the resurrection is profoundly and hauntingly nonexistent.[9] To resort

---

8   A fascinating book with this title was written by a skeptic who examined the evidence for the resurrection with the intent of destroying Christianity, but in the process became a Christian. Chapter one is titled "The Book That Refused to Be Written." See Frank Morison, *Who Moved the Stone? The Evidence for the Resurrection* (New York: Barnes & Noble, Inc., 1963). See also Parton, "The Resurrection of Jesus Christ on Trial," in *Making the Case for Christianity*, 67–92; and *The Resurrection Fact: Responding to Modern Critics*, eds. John Bombaro and Adam Francisco (Irvine: New Reformation Press, 2016), esp. 88–116, which addresses Michael Martin's arguments against the resurrection in particular and notes the number of lawyers involved in the actions surrounding that event (e.g., Nicodemus, Joseph of Arimathea, Gamaliel, and Paul).

9   As mentioned, California law allows a jury to conclude that no such counter evidence existed since the Roman and Jewish authorities had every opportunity and motivation to produce the evidence if they could. See California Evidence Code sections 412 and 413 and California Form of Jury Instruction 205[1].

to arguments found in non-eyewitness accounts arising centuries later (as in the so-called Gnostic gospels of Thomas and Judas, as well as the 7th-century Koran) would be met in any court of law with hearsay and lack of foundation objections that any noncomatose trial-court judge in America would sustain.

The fact is that the evidence for the death and resurrection of Jesus Christ is as complete and sound as any fact of the ancient world. A team of experts (including a medical doctor) writing in the *Journal of the American Medical Association*, for example, rigorously examined the evidence for the death of Jesus as described in the eyewitness accounts.[10] Their conclusion? The crucifixion of Jesus lines up precisely with what we know of first-century Roman practices. Centurions knew their business and the eyewitness accounts perfectly describe Roman procedure. This man was dead on the cross and any "defense" that he faked his death on the cross (sometimes referred to as the "swoon theory") and then miraculously revived in the tomb through the conspiratorial efforts of friends Lazarus and Joseph of Arimathea are simply incredible. More important, if Jesus did not die on the cross, both Roman and Jewish authorities would be highly motivated to proclaim that fact and were not in the least motivated to suppress the evidence.

Similarly, any notion that those same witnesses who attest to the crucifixion and death of Jesus and then to his appearance to them three days later fully alive were somehow subject to mass hypnosis is utterly untenable. Psychiatric research is clear that such mass delusion occurs only over highly unstable and short periods of time.[11] In the case of the witnesses of the risen Jesus after his crucifixion,

---

10   William D. Edwards, M.D., et al., "On the Physical Death of Jesus Christ," *The Journal of the American Medical Association* 255, no. 11 (1986): 1455–1463. Other medically trained professionals have come to the exact same conclusion. See C. Truman Davis, M.D., "The Crucifixion of Jesus: The Passion of Christ from a Medical Point of View," *Arizona Medicine* 22 (March 1965): 183–187; James H. Jewell Jr., M.D. and Patricia A. Didden, M.D., "A Surgeon Looks at the Cross," *Voice* 58, no. 2 (1979): 3–5.

11   Paul Hoch and Joseph Zubin, eds., *Psychopathology of Perception* (New York: Grune & Stratton, 1965), 18; see also Paul William Preu, M.D., *Outline of Psychiatric Casestudy: A Practical Handbook* (New York: Paul Hoeber, Inc., 1939), 97–99.

the evidence against mass delusional hysteria could not be more secure. Those appearances occur to a variety of personalities, over widely varying geographical and physical conditions, lasting over a month, and involving personalities hardly susceptible to falling sway to an ecstatic vision (like some villagers all claiming to see the face of Jesus in a particularly greasy tortilla). Many of the eyewitnesses of the resurrected Christ suffered the most repulsive and disgusting of deaths for their convictions and had every motivation to get their perception of the facts right.

We note that the number of experienced lawyers who have carefully investigated the eyewitness testimony in support of the death and resurrection of Jesus is impressive. The list of those concluding that the evidence in support of the death and resurrection of Jesus would be admissible in any common-law court in the world include Hugo Grotius, Matthew Hale, William Blackstone, Simon Greenleaf, Edmund Bennett, Jacques Ellul, Sir Norman Anderson, Lord Hailsham, and John Warwick Montgomery.[12]

Does the Existence of Evil Trump All Evidence for the Existence of God?

Finally, isn't all this talk about facts and evidence missing the point? After all, if God is so loving and good, why is there real, objective evil (e.g., the Holocaust and 9/11) and incomprehensible suffering in the world (e.g., pediatric AIDS victims)?[13] The conclusion, it is argued, could not be more clear: either God Himself is not good since if He was He would surely not allow evil in the first place; or He is not powerful enough to stop evil and suffering. Either way, it is argued, the God whose existence you have "proven" is either evil Himself or too weak to be taken seriously and powerless to defeat

---

12   Brief descriptions of the qualifications of this group are noted in chapter four, note 25. See also Ross Clifford, *Leading Lawyers' Case for the Resurrection* (Edmonton: Canadian Institute for Law, Theology, and Public Policy, 1996).

13   For the best refutation of Richard Dawkins's claim that the God of the Bible is a "bloodthirsty ethnic cleanser" and a "homophobic, racist, genocidal and sadomasochistic bully," see Paul Copan, *Is God a Moral Monster? Making Sense of the Old Testament God* (Grand Rapids: Baker Books, 2011).

evil. In sum, the evidence for God's existence must be irrelevant because it produces a God hardly worthy of worship.

First, we note a logical problem with the argument that the existence of evil disproves the existence of God. Without an *absolute* moral standard (which the analytical philosopher Ludwig Wittgenstein established is not possible without a transcendent source[14]), one cannot even speak of "evil" save in a totally relative or culturally conditioned manner. In short, one must presuppose an absolute moral standard to even employ the word *evil* in a comprehensible fashion. However, an absolute standard of morality is impossible unless God exists. If there is no God, both good and evil are strictly relative concepts and by-products of cultural conditions and sociological-political-psychological factors. If God does not exist, there is no "problem" of evil. What is is, and no more can be said.

Second, Christianity is not in the least incompatible with the existence of evil in the universe. The biblical data is unimpeachably clear that evil entered the universe through the volitional acts of the creature, not the Creator. Evil entered the human condition as a result of a completely free moral choice by the creature to do his own will in direct contradiction to the edict of God Almighty. The result was eternal separation from God, as well as suffering and death in this life. Sin is irrational, however, and does not obey nice, clean rules of cause and effect (i.e., you get only what you truly deserve). Thus, innocent children contract AIDS and innocent bystanders die in terrorist attacks.

But the biblical picture does not end simply by separating God from the cause of evil. Indeed, in Jesus Christ, death (the final result of sin and evil) is conquered decisively and forever. Jesus is furious at the tomb of Lazarus for the devastation that human evil and death bring (John 11:17–38).[15] In Christianity, a most solid foundation exists for

---

14   Ludwig Wittgenstein, in his magnum opus, *Tractatus Logico-Philosophicus*, concluded as follows in proposition 6.421: "Ethics is transcendental."

15   We also note that environmental activists associated with the United Nations are now saying that the concept of a "natural disaster" needs fundamental rethinking since environmental and resource mismanagement, despotic and corrupt human governments, and negligent or selfish human

fighting against evil and for doing so with complete confidence that this fight has the divine stamp of approval. Contrary to the attitude of benign resignation in Eastern religions toward evil (the concept of Karma and the essential unity of good and evil emasculate any real ability to aggressively counter the cause and effects of human evil and suffering), Christianity speaks of human depravity being so real and dreadful that it required the entrance into grainy human history by the sinless Son of God in order to make atonement. Thus, not only is evil condemned, but also God Himself takes on the consequences of that evil in His very body.

The result is that no one can say God does not understand human suffering and evil. The cross of Jesus, for Christianity, forever silences the argument that God does not get what it is like to be human, to suffer, to be unjustly treated, and to die. Finally, Christianity is clear that Jesus Christ will return again to totally obliterate all human suffering and evil and to wipe the tear from every eye. These facts allowed Francis Collins, one of the world's leading geneticists and longtime head of the Human Genome Project, to leave atheism for Christianity and to later maintain his Christian beliefs despite a monstrous personal evil being inflicted on his daughter.[16]

Dorothy Sayers summarizes the issue : "Christianity has compelled the mind of man not because it is the most cheering view of man's existence, but because it is truest to the facts."[17] Any worldview is inadequate that does not take evil seriously and give a foundation to aggressively combat evil. Christianity offers this unreservedly while also clearly holding forth the ultimate victory over evil. Sayers further contends, quite rightly, that Christianity is the only religion that gives not only a comprehensive understanding of the origin and

beings often either (a) are the cause of man-made disasters (fires, floods, droughts, famine), or (b) severely magnify such disasters by creating a highly vulnerable populace (hurricanes, earthquakes, tornadoes, tsunamis, volcanos wreaking havoc largely on the poorest of the poor). See Anders Wijkman and Lloyd Timberlake, *Natural Disasters: Acts of God or Acts of Man?* (Washington DC: International Institute for Environment and Development, 1984).

16   Francis S. Collins, *The Language of God* (New York: Free Press, 2006), 42–47.

17   Lord David Cecil, "True and False Values," *The Fortnightly* (March 1940): 296–303, as quoted by Dorothy L. Sayers, *The Mind of the Maker* (London: Methuen & Co., 1946), 13.

nature of evil and suffering but also its ultimate remedy. It does so not by denying its reality (as in Christian Science) nor by claiming that good consists of achieving personal spiritual enlightenment and ceasing to suffer (as seen in the teachings of classical Buddhism), but by presenting the God of the Bible as the one who ultimately enters the human picture to take on evil and suffering and to conquer it at the cross and at the empty tomb.

Where Does This Leave Us?

J.R.R. Tolkien, author of *The Lord of the Rings,* notes how the resurrection is the central verification of the Christian claim and the marriage of legend and history in a supremely historical event that has the inner consistency of "Primary Art":

> The Gospels contain . . . a story of a larger kind which embraces all the essence of fairy-stories. They contain many marvels— peculiarly artistic, beautiful, and moving; "mythical" in their perfect, self-contained significance; and at the same time powerfully symbolic and allegorical; and among the marvels, the greatest and most complete conceivable eucatastrophe. The Birth of Christ is the eucatastrophe of Man's history. The Resurrection is the eucatastrophe of the story of the Incarnation. This story begins and ends in joy. It has preeminently the "inner consistency of reality." There is no tale ever told that men would rather find was true, and none which so many skeptical men have accepted as true on its own merits. For the Art of it has the supremely convincing tone of Primary Art, that is, of Creation. To reject it leads either to sadness or to wrath.[18]

---

18   J.R.R. Tolkien, *On Fairy Stories: Essays Presented to Charles Williams* (London: Oxford University Press, 1947), 83–84. Reprinted by permission of HarperCollins Publishers Ltd © J.R.R. Tolkien 1947.

We now want to turn to look at the consequences of this religion being, in fact, true. If it has the value of being what Tolkien calls "Primary Art," this should have both social and cultural implications, as well as provide a foundation for personal validation of its claims.

"*A single sentence will suffice for modern man: He fornicated and he read the papers.*"

—ALBERT CAMUS[1]

---

1   *The Fall*, 6.

CHAPTER SIX

Christianity May Be True, but Does It Even *Matter?*

A religion like Christianity may be, as a matter of fact, *true*. However, it may still have no substantive *value* for matters of this life and this world. That is the issue we will now address.

So far we have discussed why, as a matter of *fact* and as far as the truth-determining process is involved, the Christian truth claims are verifiable and evidentially supportable. But a correct and factually accurate worldview should have practical, real-world *value* for the individual and for culture in general. This is, fortunately, precisely the case with Christianity. The evidence to establish the value of Christianity for the individual in this world, and for culture at large, is simply overwhelming in its richness.

Even the most basic analysis of the condition of the world confronts us with certain unalterable facts about the human condition. Without any serious question, man's depravity toward his fellow man is writ large. It is broadcast to us daily through newspapers, television, film, and theater. Christianity, while promising a new life in Christ, never suggests that this world will be transformed into "heaven on earth" as long as sinful people are here.[2] It is, in a word, realistic about human depravity. No Christian should ever be shocked by what he or she reads in the daily papers about man's inhumanity to man. It is the secularist who must be constantly disappointed with each day's headlines of wars and rumors of wars, man wreaking havoc on man.

Similarly, the Christian worldview looks very disfavorably on efforts to wall off the Christian from secular society in order to prevent "moral pollution." Such efforts are chronicled in history as general catastrophes. One only has to read the long history of failed efforts at Christian communalism to see this in bold relief. While monasticism certainly had some advantages in being the birthplace, for example, of the modern university, the separatism and internal moral hierarchy it created had no biblical support. The first Christians integrated completely into their society and literally "turned the world upside down" (Acts 17:6) with the message of the empty tomb.

However, if the Christian conception of the universe and man's situation is, as a matter of fact, true and correct as presented in the primary source material, one obtains a foundation for taking human sin and misery seriously, for combating evil in this world since it does not originate with God, and for advancing man both intellectually and physically since he is "fearfully and wonderfully made" (Psalm 139:14). That has, in fact, been precisely the case in the history of Christianity's impact on culture as can be illustrated in literally countless ways.

Christianity and the Effort to Relieve Human Suffering

For example, human evil and suffering was in fact confronted directly and aggressively by Jesus Christ Himself (He is even referred to in classical theology as "The Great Physician"). Consequently, Christianity gave birth to the rise of modern medicine and the establishment of the first hospitals, including care for the mentally

---

2   The Apostle John puts it very forcefully: "If we say we have not sinned, we make Him [God] a liar" (1 John 1:10); and Jesus asserts that "No one is good except God alone" (Mark 10:18).

ill.[3] In addition, the church-run convent gave rise to the profession of nursing and was greatly reformed and advanced by the efforts of Florence Nightingale, a devout Christian. The Red Cross has its origins in Christianity, and Christians are also credited for the beginning of orphanages and homes for the elderly. The ecumenical council of the Christian Church at Nicaea in 325 directed the bishops to establish a hospice in every city that had a cathedral.[4]

It is true that the Greek and Roman worlds practiced medicine, but treatment was clearly based on ability to pay and there was essentially no concept of caring for the poor or mentally ill. Eastern societies simply had no philosophical basis to combat evil or to develop a robust approach to medicine and health care, since it was seen as part of Karma or denied as contrary to ultimate reality, which is found when one's enlightenment results in the actual cessation of suffering.[5]

Christianity puts strong value on each individual being created in the image of God. Rich or poor, day laborer or President of a Fortune 500 company, all stand as equal before the God of Christian revelation. In contrast, Greek and Roman societies elevated their leaders and citizens to a higher place than all others and had little concern for the poor and sick. Extending charity to the sick and poor has never been a trait of either paganism or highly rationalistic societies.[6] Yet Christianity introduced the idea of the value of all human beings and the need to care "for the least of these" (Matthew 25:40). This is

---

3   Alvin J. Schmidt, *Under the Influence: How Christianity Transformed Civilization* (Grand Rapids: Zondervan, 2001), 156. A sampling of Schmidt's chapter headings is instructive: "The Sanctification of Human Life," "Christianity Elevates Sexual Morality," "Women Receive Freedom and Dignity," "Hospitals and Health Care: Their Christian Roots," "Christianity's Imprint on Education," "Labor and Economic Freedom Dignified," and "Slavery Abolished: A Christian Achievement."

4   Nathaniel W. Faxon, *The Hospital in Contemporary Life* (Cambridge: Harvard University Press, 1949), 7.

5   For example, see Edward Ryan, *The History of the Effects of Religion on Mankind: In Countries Ancient and Modern, Barbarous and Civilized* (Dublin: T.M. Bates, 1802), 268: "The bonzas or Japanese priests, for instance, by maintaining that the sick and needy were odious to the gods, prevented the rich from relieving them."

6   A.R. Hands, *Charities and Social Aid in Greece and Rome* (Ithaca: Cornell University Press, 1968), 27–28ff.

why even the concept of a "Christian terrorist-suicide bomber" is utterly absurd.

The world has yet to know an atheist leper colony or an agnostic orphanage. Atheism and scientific materialism provide utterly no intellectual foundation for the combating of human misery. What is is. Contrary to the Eastern religions with their doctrines of Karma and withdrawal from desire and the temptations of this world, Christians have been in the forefront of the development of all means possible to attack and relieve human suffering.

Christianity and the Value of the Intellect

In a similar manner, Christianity has valued the life of the mind and the development of human artistic endeavor from its earliest days. Not only is the modern university the product of a Christian conception of the universe[7] as well as the product of the efforts of the monasteries to systematize learning (the assumption being that all knowledge is interrelated), but also the rise of public and compulsory education itself was directly a product of the Reformation's activities in Germany and its commitment to teach every ploughboy to read the Bible for himself.[8]

Christianity put a unique emphasis on universal education. Jews were known as "People of the Book," and Christianity continued this tradition by encouraging the widespread copying and studying of the Christian Scriptures. Being learned in the Scriptures and in the ancient languages that informed Scripture (Hebrew, Greek, and Latin) became critical. In fact, the so-called "humanist" Renaissance was actually led almost solely by solidly believing Christians (Dante,

---

7   Over 90% of all the colleges and universities existing in this country before the Civil War were founded by Christian denominations. See Donald Tewksbury, *The Founding of American Colleges and Universities before the Civil War* (New York: Teachers College, Columbia University Press, 1932), 82.

8   G. Forell, H. Grimm, and T. Hoelty-Nickel, *Luther and Culture* (Decorah, IA: Luther College Press, 1960). See especially the section titled "Luther and Education," 73–142; see also Schmidt, *Under the Influence*, 170–193, for a discussion of the Christian roots of education for the deaf and blind.

Petrarch, Boccaccio, Pico della Mirandola, da Vinci, Michelangelo, and Erasmus) and was truly a Christian movement.[9] It is well established that the Reformation's emphasis on literacy and learning led directly to the development of libraries and highlighted the importance of broad learning in the arts and sciences.[10]

In Greece and Roman societies, a liberal education was only available for boys from privileged classes. Girls and noncitizens received, at most, vocational training.[11] Christianity, on the other hand, introduced a very strong emphasis on universal education, including education for girls and for the poor. Monasteries developed education in the liberal arts. During the Middle Ages, cathedral schools for boys and girls taught the seven liberal arts, including the *trivium* (grammar, rhetoric, and logic) and the *quadrivium* (arithmetic, music, geometry, and astronomy).

As noted, the Reformation put even greater emphasis on cultivating literate laity who could read the Bible for themselves. Martin Luther realized there could be no permanent reformation without a reformation in education, and thus he called for public school education.[12]

Serious Christians have been leading lights in the development of the educated mind. Johannes Sturm (1507–1589) introduced the idea of graded education and developed the idea of the humanistic *Gymnasium* in Strasbourg in 1538, while Friedrich Fröbel (1782–1852) originated the kindergarten. It was Christians, too, who developed

---

9   Stanford historian of the Renaissance Lewis Spitz makes this clear in his classic two-volume work on the period. See *The Renaissance and Reformation Movements* (Chicago: Rand McNally & Co., 1972), 1:139ff.

10   Alfred Hessel, *A History of Libraries*, trans. Reuben Peiss (Washington DC: Scarecrow Press, 1950), 51: "The Reformation forms an epoch in the history of libraries." See also John Warwick Montgomery, "Luther, Libraries, and Learning," reprinted in Montgomery's *In Defense of Martin Luther* (Milwaukee: Northwestern, 1970), 116–139, which explains how Luther's basic theological thrust motivated the establishment and flourishing of libraries.

11   Kenneth J. Freeman, *Schools of Hellas: An Essay on the Practice and Theory of Ancient Greek Education From 600 to 300 B.C.* (London: Macmillan, 1922), 46.

12   Martin Luther, "To the Councilmen of All Cities in Germany That They Establish and Maintain Christian Schools," in Luther's Works, trans. Albert T.W. Steinhauser; ed. Robert Schultz (Philadelphia: Fortress Press, 1967), 45:344.

schools for the deaf using sign language, while the Christian Louis Braille developed the system of raised dots so that the blind could read.[13]

Christianity and Science

There is a long and distinguished history of serious Christian involvement in the scientific enterprise. The foundation for this effort was the conviction that the universe reflects a rational and intelligent Creator and that intelligence is built into the universe.[14] In addition, the Christian conception of the universe (unlike animism, pantheism, and the Eastern religions) posits a God who created the world and yet is separate and distinct from it. Alfred North Whitehead, the renowned philosopher of science, goes so far as to say that the origin of science required Christianity's "insistence on the rationality of God."[15] In short, a correct worldview about nature itself is required in order to conclude that nature is congenial to systematic study. If the universe is fundamentally random or illusory, it is inevitable that such an impoverished view of nature will tend toward what Stanley Jaki, a philosopher of science, says are "stillbirths" and stagnation in science.[16]

By distinguishing the Creator from the creation while still retaining the view that creation was good even if not "one with God," Christianity removed the pagan and Greek tendency to deify nature. This made the study of nature morally permissible while also giving a foundation for the goodness of matter—after all, Jesus Himself had made matter sacred by taking the form of man.[17]

---

13   Harlan Lane, *When the Mind Hears* (New York: Random House, 1984), 58.

14   Johannes Kepler, the 16th-century astronomer, put it nicely: "To God there are, in the whole material world, material laws, figures and relations of special excellency and of the most appropriate order. . . . Those laws are within the grasp of the human mind; God wanted us to recognize them by creating us after his own image so that we could share his own thoughts" (Letter to Herwart von Hohenburg in 1599, reprinted in Carola Baumgardt, *Johannes Kepler: Life and Letters* [New York: Philosophical Library, 1951], 50).

15   Alfred North Whitehead, *Science and the Modern World* (New York: Macmillan, 1926), 18.

16   Stanley Jaki, *The Savior of Science* (Grand Rapids: Eerdmans, 2000), 28.

17   Jaki, *The Savior of Science*, 79–81.

Thus, if God is a rational being, then human beings made in His image may also employ their rational faculties to study and investigate the world in which they find themselves. The inductive process, fundamental to scientific inquiry, was thus blessed by the Christian revelation and was instrumental in releasing the stranglehold of Aristotelian pantheism, which controlled scientific endeavor for 1,500 years and was based in large part on the confidence that knowledge was best determined by the deductive processes of the mind.[18]

The list of those involved in this endeavor who were also serious Christian believers is legion and includes, among others, Francis Bacon (the practical creator of scientific induction), Nicolaus Copernicus (proposed the heliocentric theory), Tycho Brahe (discovered a new comet and built an observatory), Johannes Kepler (discovered elliptical movement of the planets, developed and confirmed three astronomical laws, was the first scientist to define weight as the mutual attraction between two bodies, and was instrumental in establishing the heliocentric theory), Galileo (first to use the telescope to study the universe and observed, among other things, lunar mountains), Blaise Pascal (discovered that liquid in a container exerts equal pressure in all directions and that barometric pressures vary with different altitudes), Isaac Newton (discovered the law of gravity and invented calculus independently of Leibniz, who was also a Christian believer), Robert Boyle (discovered Boyle's law, namely that the volume of gas varies inversely with its pressure), Michael Faraday (discovered electromagnetic induction), Louis Pasteur (founded microbiology) and Gregor Mendel (laid the foundation for modern genetics).[19]

Christianity and Valuing the Arts

In the realm of artistic and musical accomplishments, the Western tradition in art and music (i.e., Bach,[20] Handel, Mendelssohn, Brahms,

---

18   Jaki, *The Savior of Science*, 41ff.

19   Schmidt, *Under the Influence*, 240–241.

20   Bach's colossal musical output (contained in 171 CDs) is simply not understandable without appreciating his serious theological commitment grounded in the truths recovered in the Lutheran

Michelangelo, Dürer, Rembrandt, Rouault, the cathedrals of Europe, cantatas, plainsong, and polyphonic and classical music[21]—the list is literally endless) is unexplainable without appealing to the Christian worldview of its creators.

Christianity provided the foundation for the arts and music to flourish. Being created in the *imago Dei*, each human being is unique and has (contrary to impersonal or monistic Eastern religions) profound creative gifts that are not to be stuffed in a corner and ignored. Neither are these gifts to be used merely to give the public what it wants nor what it will buy. Biblical theology gives the strongest encouragement to develop those gifts and to use the vocations of artist and musician to both glorify God and to edify and build up one's neighbor (as opposed to merely titillating or shocking the audience or massaging one's artistic ego).[22]

In short, worldview determines how one sees the world and what one wants to do with respect to the human condition.

Christianity also offers personal and experiential validation of its claims. The list of lives transformed by a personal relationship with Jesus Christ is impressive.[23] We cite this not to ground the truth of Christianity's claim in subjective experience (an effort we have gone

---

Reformation. See the many sources in this regard cited in full at Parton, *The Defense Never Rests*, 141–147; Parton, "Christian Liberty, the Arts, and J.S. Bach," in *Where Christ Is Present: A Theology for All Seasons on the 500th Anniversary of the Reformation*, eds. John Warwick Montgomery and Gene Edward Veith (Irvine: New Reformation Press, 2015), 165–192.

21   One need only try to figure out what great classical composer did not set the Western liturgical rite known as "the Mass" to music. For many musicians, the Mass is widely considered their crowning achievement. Three examples from the kings of classical music should suffice to establish the point: Bach's Mass in B Minor (which many commentators consider the greatest piece of music ever conceived), Mozart's Mass in C Minor, and Beethoven's Mass in D Major (which he wrote near the end of his life and yet called it "the greatest work that I have written"—see "A Commentary on the Missa Solemnis, Op. 123," by Monika Lichtenfeld, found in Ludwig van Beethoven, *Missa Solemnis in D, Op. 123*, with the Bach-Collegium Stuttgart and Gächinger Kantorei Stuttgart, conducted by Helmuth Rilling, Hänssler Classic CD 98.053, 1997, compact disc).

22   Bach, for example, believed the theological foundation for all God-pleasing church music was provided in the Old Testament Book of Chronicles where, among other things, the position of Church Musician was created to offer instrumental and vocal gifts as part of the worship service in the tabernacle. See Robin A. Leaver, *J.S. Bach and Scripture* (St. Louis: Concordia Publishing House, 1985), 93–94—noting Bach's handwritten notes in the margin of his Bible relating to 1 Chronicles 25.

23   For a work by a host of serious French Christians detailing their conversions to Christianity and its impact on their respective academic and professional fields, see Françoise Bluche, *Pourquoi Croyez-vous en Dieu? [Why Do You Believe in God?]* (Paris: Criterion Books, 1994).

to some lengths to show is most dangerous) but to point the serious inquirer to the fact that Jesus proclaimed Himself as the Prince of Peace. There are legions of individuals who attest to the personal peace with God and then with their fellow man which has followed from their commitment to Jesus Christ.

Christianity and Human Rights

Some argue that Christianity, even if "true," results in a position of maximum cultural irrelevance. Why? Because of the absence of Christian intellectual and moral activity in our day relating to the major human rights abuses of our time (the domain is largely inhabited by secularists with vague and contradictory notions of "social justice"). Indeed, we live in an age where such "justice" issues are constantly being discussed and debated often without *any* contribution by serious Christians. Never before has there been more concern about "human rights" as is witnessed by the rise of international tribunals relating to human rights violations based in Strasbourg, France, with its counterpart in The Hague, Netherlands; and yet never before does our own day provide almost daily examples of the most deplorable treatment of other human beings through acts of genocide and terror (think Rwanda, the former Yugoslavia, ISIS activities throughout the world, civil rights abuses in North Korea and China, etc.).

Though we live in the most advanced of times in many ways, sadly the respect for basic human rights throughout the world is objectively deplorable. Just one illustration of this fact: there are more people subject today to human slavery and trafficking than at any time in the history of the world![24]

The problem is not that people oppose "human rights" in principle—few do.[25] Almost everyone (including dictators) favors his or

---

24   See Justice Dallas Miller, "The Motivation to Protect and Advance Human Rights," in *Legitimizing Human Rights: Secular and Religious Perspectives*, ed. Angus Menuge (Surrey, England: Ashgate Publishing Company, 2013), 188–189.

25   The United Nations foundational document on the topic (the "Universal Declaration of Human Rights") was adopted by the UN General Assembly on December 10, 1948, by *unanimous* vote. See Miller, "The Motivation to Protect and Advance Human Rights," 183.

her own self-advantageous notion of "human rights." The problem is twofold: (1) sufficiently justifying the source and specific content of human rights so that they are not subjective and culturally relative but instead objective and cross-cultural and thus universal and "inalienable"; and (2) changing the condition of the human heart to *want* to protect human rights because what the field needs is not simply more good advice about human rights.

The paths in law and legal philosophy to justify and ground universal human rights are essentially two-fold: (1) the notion that absolute human rights are derivable from man's nature and are therefore universally recognized by all cultures across time and supported by the human conscience (the so-called "natural law" approach to justifying human rights); and (2) that genuine human rights only derive from the legal system of individual nations or societies and that the quest for universal human rights that are cross-cultural is utterly futile. This view (known as "legal realism") allows criticism of any system of human rights but only from within the system itself—that is, the system can be criticized but only for being internally inconsistent with its own principles and structure.

Natural law theory goes back as far as the Greeks and Romans (Aristotle, Cicero, and Seneca speak to it), and it was essentially formally incorporated into Christian theology by Thomas Aquinas in the Middle Ages. It was the dominant view undergirding any concept of human rights until the 19th century. It was refined or modified during the 18th-century Enlightenment, and its concept of "inalienable rights" made it into the founding documents of the United States as well as into the Declaration of the Rights of Man in France in the 18th century.[26] The essence of natural law theory over almost 2,000 years is that built into human beings is an absolute morality or a universal law written on the human heart and conscience.[27]

---

26   We will not be addressing current efforts along the so-called "neo-Kantian" lines—John Rawls and Alan Gewirth being its primary exponents—to develop an absolute and rationally derived ethic without needing the existence of God and by formulating variations on Kant's "categorical imperative," which says each person should "act as if his action could become a universal norm."

27   See Paul Copan, "Grounding Human Rights," in *Legitimizing Human Rights*, 11–31; Thom-

CHAPTER SIX | CHRISTIANITY MAY BE TRUE, BUT DOES IT EVEN MATTER?

What is the problem with this theory? There are at least three overwhelming difficulties with "natural law" defenses of universal human rights.

First, this view results in ambiguity in the precise content of any particular human right. One illustration will suffice: The Justinian Code is the great law code of the 6th century that "codified" aspects of Roman law up to that point. That code defines three universal principles of human conduct: (1) To live honestly (*Honeste vivere*); (2) to harm no one (*Alterum non laedere*); and (3) to make sure each person gets what he or she legitimately deserves (*Suum cuique tribuere*). Fine. Who can argue with that? We are compelled to note, though, that the third prong of this ethical code was explicitly and consciously incorporated by the Nazis in WWII, translated into German (*Jedem das Seine*—"to each his proper due"), and placed on the front gates of the death camp at Buchenwald and other Nazi concentration camps. For the Nazis, gassing 6 million Jews was "giving" "to each his proper due" and was consistent with the dictates of the Justinian Code.

Second, the natural law theory of justifying human rights commits what we noted in a previous chapter and what philosopher G.E. Moore referred to as the "naturalistic fallacy" (or "sociological fallacy" as it is often called). This logical fallacy consists of thinking that one can move from the "is" of this world and what people are actually doing to the "ought" of universal ethics without further justification. Just because the ruling Nazi party in the 1940s in fact treated the Jewish population as subhuman and worthy of extermination hardly proves the ethic of that despicable action. In addition, natural law theory commits the related logical fallacy of *consensus gentium,* or the idea that because almost everyone agrees about something at any particular time in history, that somehow makes it true.[28] But in

---

as Johnson, *Natural Law Ethics* (Bonn, Germany: Culture and Science Publ., 2005), 128–140; J. Budziszewski, "Accept No Imitations: The Rivalry of Naturalism and Natural Law," in *Uncommon Dissent: Intellectuals Who Find Darwinism Unconvincing,* ed. William A. Dembski (Wilmington, DE: ISI Books, 2004), 99–113.

28 This fallacy has been noted as particularly prevalent in the process known as "peer review" in

the Middle Ages almost everyone thought that the sun went around the earth (the geocentric system advocated since Ptolemy in the 2nd century A.D.) until the heliocentric system was proven in the experimentation of people like Copernicus and Kepler in the 16th and 17th centuries.[29]

Third, there is no such consensus anyway on the content of so-called "natural law rights" that are supposedly built into human nature! The extraordinary diversity of what is believed about the most basic of human rights (e.g., the value of human beings as a unique species) came to particular light as anthropologists studied extinct and existing foreign and non-Western cultures. Cannibals have an ethic of "leave no femurs on your plate," while Buddhism was hardly tolerant of Roman Catholic missionaries.[30] Aztec culture engaged in human sacrifice and the modern Ik tribal people of Northeastern Uganda force their children as young as 3 to leave home and live in gangs to find their own food. Adult males and fathers in the Ik tribe will gorge themselves on hunted game while watching even their own small children starve to death.[31]

The point is that there is tremendous diversity in both historical and current cultural value systems, and even if you could prove there was consensus on major human rights issues across cultures and across time, it hardly proves their moral rightness. Furthermore, natural right theory for justifying human rights has embedded in it a seemingly naive view of human nature. Even the 17th-century atheist Thomas Hobbes quite rightly noted that the human condition is "nasty, brutish, and short," and failing to account for radical self-centeredness in human beings leads to wildly divergent notions

---

modern science scholarship where such review often hardens into blindly enforcing the current orthodoxy and penalizes or retards real innovation and scientific discovery. See Frank J. Tipler, "Refereed Journals: Do They Insure Quality or Enforce Orthodoxy?," in *Uncommon Dissent*, 115–130.

29   John Lennox, *Seven Days That Divide the World: The Beginning According to Genesis and Science* (Grand Rapids: Zondervan, 2011), 15–20.

30   See Martin Scorsese's 2016 film *Silence* for a disturbing view of 17th-century Japanese Buddhism's horrific treatment of Christians in general.

31   The classic work on the tribe is Colin M. Turnbull's *The Mountain People* (New York: Simon & Schuster, 1970).

of what is "natural" and what truly violates some supposed cross-cultural and universal notion of "conscience."

The inadequacies of the natural right position as a foundation for universal human rights led philosopher Jeremy Bentham in the 19th century to call it "nonsense upon stilts,"[32] meaning that human beings were naively thinking they could lift themselves above their actual human level to come up with absolute universal rights. The legal realists found such efforts totally inadequate. The only genuine rights were those established by governments (or any other sovereign including dictators) and by individual societies. If the nation, sovereign, or society espouses ethical principles and its system is at least internally consistent, no further judgment can be offered. Law could never be connected to eternal verities.[33]

But legal realism has been found unable to condemn even the most deplorable atrocities from any source outside the confines of the particular society or nation being analyzed. Thus when WWII concluded and the famous Nuremberg War Crimes trials were conducted, German defense counsel for Goering, Hess, Speer, and Company argued on strictly "legal realism" grounds that no universally recognized law or "higher law" could stand in judgment of the Nazi's position on the Jews. Looking strictly at the German legal code of the time, the Nazi perpetrators acted consistently with German law as it then existed.[34] Not surprising, legal realism has been found

---

32   Jeremy Bentham, *Rights, Representation, and Reform: Nonsense Upon Stilts and Other Writings on the French Revolution*, ed. P. Schofield, et al. (Oxford: Oxford University Press, 2002), 317–401.

33   19th-century English legal theorist John Austin put it this way: "Law is the dictate of the Sovereign"; while the former Associate Justice of the United States Supreme Court Oliver Wendell Holmes believed "[a] law should be called good if it reflects the will of the dominant forces of the community even if it will take us to hell" (Holmes to fellow Justice Felix Frankfurter in a letter dated March 24, 1914, in *Holmes and Frankfurter: Their Correspondence,*1912–1934, eds. Robert Mennel and Christine Compston [Hanover: University Press of New England, 1996], 19). Thus Albert Alschuler's biography of Holmes is fittingly titled: *Law Without Values: The Life, Work, and Legacy of Justice Holmes* (Chicago: University of Chicago Press, 2000).

34   Chief Prosecutor and United States Associate Supreme Court Justice Robert Jackson attempted to justify the trials by appealing to "the basic principles of jurisprudence which are the assumptions of civilization." See Robert Jackson, "Closing Address in the Nuremberg Trial," in *Trial of the Major War Criminals before the International Military Tribunal*, vol. 19 (Nuremberg, Germany: International Military Tribunal, 1948), 397. For a trenchant critique of the questionable foundation

incapable of providing justification for the condemnation of human right abuses in Third World and Eastern societies.

Thus, natural right theory has been found wanting and incapable of providing a defensible basis for human rights, while legal realism is equally incapable of providing anything but a relative and culturally derived standard of judgment on human rights.

So, where does one go from here? We see that the human-generated efforts at justifying human rights have been tried and found wanting and that a defensible grounding for universal human rights is critical. However, we have previously seen that one cannot obtain absolutes from non-absolute sources, and yet it is necessary for that source or sources to originate outside the human condition.[35] We see that everyone wants human rights and "supports" them in concept, that everyone condemns behavior they think is deplorable, and that any answer to the problem of justifying human rights must come from outside the human condition. The human race is in the same place the Greek philosopher Archimedes was in during second-century B.C. Athens. Archimedes, who discovered the principle of the displacement of water and is considered the greatest mathematician and mechanical engineer of all antiquity,[36] said that if he had a lever long enough and a fulcrum outside the world, he could move the world with the touch of his finger. Renowned 20th-century analytical philosopher Ludwig Wittgenstein says the same thing but more dynamically: "If a man could write a book on Ethics which really was a book on Ethics, this book would, with an explosion, destroy all the other books in the world."[37]

---

for Jackson's argument, see John Warwick Montgomery, *Defending the Gospel in Legal Style* (Bonn, Germany: Culture and Science Publ., 2017), 133–35.

35   As 18th-century French philosopher Jean-Jacques Rousseau put it, "In order to discover the rules of society best suited to nations, a superior intelligence beholding all the passions of men without experiencing any of them would be needed. This intelligence would have to be wholly unrelated to our nature, while knowing it through and through; its happiness would have to be independent of us, and yet ready to occupy itself with ours; and lastly, it would have, in the march of time, to look forward to a distant glory, and, working in one century, to be able to enjoy in the next. *It would take gods to give men laws*" (*On the Social Contract* [1762], Bk. 2, Ch. 7, emphasis added).

36   Benjamin Farrington, *Greek Science*, rev. ed. (Harmondsworth, Middlesex: Penguin, 1961), 214.

37   "A Lecture on Ethics," *Philosophical Review* 74 (January 1965): 7.

In short, we need a transcendent source for universal human rights to have any meaningfulness. If there is no God, there is no defensible basis for human rights. But we need more than the existence of God. If that existent God has not communicated ultimate values to us as humans in a propositional or understandable form, that God's general existence is of little value in the discussion of human rights.

We have already seen that merely making claims to be a transcendent source and to have spoken to humanity is not unique to Christianity (Islam, Mormonism, etc. claim the same advantages). But making a claim is not the same as giving verifiable evidence of the legitimacy of that claim, and only Christianity pins its truth claims on a particular historical event happening (i.e., the resurrection). Christianity, though, not only provides that fulcrum Archimedes noted as utterly critical, and not only has that book that Wittgenstein yearned for that explodes all other books, but it also provides direction and guidance for some of the thorniest problems in human rights (e.g., the value of all human beings from conception to the end of life, the value of women, the importance of the institution of marriage for the stability of a society, the importance of maintaining a free society where people can choose to believe or not believe without suffering the loss of civil rights, the importance of civil liberties in general)[38] and promises a changed heart from within that learns to actually want to see these universal truths advanced for the betterment of society.

And there is ample evidence that Christians with changed hearts have forever changed the landscape of human rights. Take just two examples: First, the abolition of the slave trade in the British Empire in the 18th and 19th centuries has been demonstrably shown to be the result of the efforts of Christians like William Wilberforce, Granville Sharp, John Wesley, and John Newton.[39] Second, Mother

---

38   For a thorough discussion of these rights and the specific propositional support for them in that book Wittgenstein hoped for, see in general John Warwick Montgomery, *Human Rights and Human Dignity* (Grand Rapids: Zondervan, 1986), esp. 168–169.

39   "Among the evils, corrected or subdued, either by the general influence of Christianity on the minds of men, or by particular associations of Christians, the African Slave trade appears to me

Teresa's work with the Missionaries of Charity in Kolkata (formerly Calcutta), India shows, once again, that Christianity is not just another "philosophy" but instead provides the interior motivation to put the needs of others before one's own. The explicit foundation for Mother Teresa's work with "the poorest of the poor" (including adopting unwanted infants and treating all with dignity from the moment of conception through death and at no cost) was Jesus' admonition that "as you did it to one of the least of these My brothers, you did it to Me" (Matthew 25:40).[40]

When it comes to human rights, the world does not need more good advice—it needs good news. The good news is God is there and is not silent, and that He promises a new life to those who come to Him—a new life that puts the needs of others before one's own relentless self-interest.

---

to have occupied the foremost place" (Thomas Clarkson, *The History of the Rise, Progress, and Accomplishment of the Abolition of the African Slave-trade by the British Parliament*, 2 vols. [London: Frank Cass, 1968, originally published in 1808], see esp. 1:8–9). This work by Clarkson is a classic in its field and was written by one who devoted his life to opposing slavery on an international scale.

40   Mother Teresa committed her life to relieving the suffering of the poor in her immediate life and not by trying to change governmental structures through political means or trying to eradicate poverty on some grandiose global scale. In this regard, she recounts the telling story of being invited to address a world conference in Mumbai (formerly Bombay) on the plight of the poor. She was late in getting to the conference because she encountered a dying man at the entrance to the conference center. Rather than go in to participate in conference activities, she cared for the man in his dying hours. This same man, presumably, had been bypassed by countless "professional advocates for the poor" that very same day. See Mother Teresa, *Words to Live By* (Notre Dame, IN: Ave Maria Press, 1983), 25.

"I therefore believe myself to have found, on all essential points, the final solution of the problems [in philosophy]. And if I am not mistaken in this belief, then the second thing in which the value of this work consists is that it shows how little is achieved when these problems are solved."

—LUDWIG WITTGENSTEIN[1]

---

1   Wittgenstein, *Tractatus Logico-Philosophicus*, 5.

From Wittgenstein to Bach

The universe does not contain within it an adequate explanation for its existence. Philosophy, as Wittgenstein concluded, cannot generate a word from outside the human condition, let alone a word from God. Yet it is transcendence that we need and sometimes directly experience,[2] not only to ground ethics and a defensible theory of human dignity and human rights, but also to give our lives and our relationships value. Otherwise, as Hobbes says, life is "nasty, brutish, and short." However, even transcendence and a written word from God is not enough if no change in the essential human bent to be self-centered is offered. As stated earlier, what the world does *not* need more of is good advice. The world needs good news—that is, a diagnosis of its fundamental disease and the offering of a totally sufficient remedy to heal that disease.

It is possible, of course, that we are a product of a gigantic cosmic accident (Carl Sagan, Stephen Hawking, Richard Dawkins), and that

---

2   "All men have experienced the deathlessness of childhood and we may assume, that, even if only once or twice, all men have experienced transcendent joy in adulthood. Under the aspect of inductive faith, religion is the final vindication of childhood and of joy, and of all gestures that replicate these" (Peter Berger, *A Rumor of Angels: Modern Society and the Rediscovery of the Supernatural* [Garden City, NJ: Doubleday, 1969], 75). Excerpts from *A Rumor of Angels: Modern Society and the Rediscovery of the Supernatural* by Peter L. Berger, copyright © 1969 by Peter L. Berger.

morality and ethics are utterly relative (genocide and human trafficking are simply unfortunate sociology, but not intrinsically evil as judged by any eternal or universal standard). Similarly, God may exist but may be silent, and so that existence is of no value in this life.

But what if God exists and has not been silent, and what if a solution to the "curved in" condition of the human heart is offered? It would behoove anyone to check out the evidence for God's existence[3] and especially to take seriously any claims that God has entered human history; that He indeed understands our predicament, gives an answer to human suffering and evil, and desires ardently above all else our salvation from both cosmic and personal rebellion. If that has happened, it would be the greatest news ever.

Our study of religions leads to an inescapable conclusion: the world's religions are not one and are not speaking with a common voice. The world's religions do not support the claim that there are many paths up the same mountain. The paths are utterly inimical to one another on almost every important issue. In fact, the world's religions disagree about the existence and nature of the mountain itself and contradict one another on all of the topics of greatest importance. One simply must investigate those claims to determine which religions can withstand rigorous scrutiny. Nothing less than eternity may be at stake. Revealingly, the world's religions in general (with one important exception) do not make factual claims at all but reduce to subjective approaches for peace of mind and general "enlightenment."[4]

---

3   We have scrupulously avoided setting forth the so-called "traditional proofs for the existence of God" only because the arguments do not proceed inductively but deductively. One should not assume, however, that those arguments are invalid. Quite the contrary. For example, the contingency argument for the existence of God is extremely powerful, and its validity alone was sufficient for renowned British philosopher and legendary atheist Antony Flew to renounce atheism and become a theist. Flew also was impressed with the essentially irreducible complexity of the universe at the microbiological level. See the interview of Flew by Dr. Gary Habermas, "My Pilgrimage from Atheism to Theism," *Philosophia Christi* 6, no. 2 (2004), http://digitalcommons.liberty.edu/cgi/viewcontent.cgi?article=1336&context=lts_fac_pubs.

4   In John Updike's tragic novel about supposed Eastern-generated bliss and nirvana experienced by finding that all reality is Maya, or an illusion, the protagonist, after running through an expensive buffet line of Eastern-inspired and ultimately dead-end practices at an Oregon ashram (including Rolfing, organic massage, dynamic meditation, primal scream, rasamandalis or Krishna-

J.S. Bach's Cantata BWV 78[5] expresses the human condition with piercing honesty and suggests that Wittgenstein's desired "transcendent answer" has not only entered history but also addresses those deeds of darkness fomented first in the human heart resulting in death, and promises a new beginning in this life and ultimately a glorious future in the next:

---

based orgy practices, etc.), says, "All these therapies . . . are just a way of turning a sick person over in bed" (*S.: A Novel* [New York: Alfred A. Knopf, 1988], 136–137).

5   The renowned Bach scholar Robert Marshall calls this particular Cantata (especially the opening chorale) "one of Bach's most complex creations—a compositional *tour de force*" that reflects no less than five distinct principles of organization, including a modern Italian concerto based on a French dance suite, a 17th-century passacaglia, and a polyphonic motet, and yet "at another level the movement is a German Lutheran chorale in *Barform: AAB*—writ very large indeed" (Robert L. Marshall, *The Music of Johann Sebastian Bach: The Sources, the Style, the Significance* [New York: Prentice Hall, 1989], 78–79).

Jesu, der du meine Seele	Jesus, thou who dost take my soul
hast durch deinen bittern Tod	and by thy bitter death
aus des Teufels finstern Höhle	didst from the devil's dark abyss
und der schweren Seelennot	and from the spirit's sore distress
kräftiglich herausgerissen	powerfully wrest it free
und mich solches lassen wissen	and give me to know this
durch dein angenehmes Wort,	by thy gracious Word;
sei doch itzt, o Gott, mein Hort!	be thou now, of God, my refuge.
…Mein Wille trachtet nur nach Bösen.	…My will aspires to naught but evil.
Der Geist zwar spricht: ach! wer wird mich erlösen?	My spirit may say, Ah, who will redeem me?
Aber Fleisch und Blut zu zwingen	But to overcome flesh and blood
und das Gute zu vollbringen,	and bring goodness to fulfillment
ist über alle meine Kraft.	is beyond my power.
Will ich den Schaden nicht verhehlen,	Though I would not hide my wrongs,
so kann ich nicht, wie oft ich fehle, zählen.	I cannot count how often I err
Drum nehm ich nun der Sünden Schmerz und Pein	and so I take the pain and grief of sin,
und meiner Sorgen Bürde,	and the burden of my sorrows,
so mir sonst unerträglich würde,	which I no way else could bear,
ich liefre sie dir, Jesu, seufzend ein.	and bring them, Jesus, with sighing breath to thee.
…Dies mein Herz, mit Leid vermenget,	…This, my heart, with sorrow commingled,
so dein teures Blut besprenget,	washed in thy most precious blood
so am Kreuz vergossen ist,	that was shed on the cross,
geb ich dir, Herr Jesu Christ.	I give to thee, Lord Jesus Christ.[6]

---

6   "Jesu, der du meine Seele," BWV 78:1, 3, 5, from The Bach Ensemble, Joshua Rifkin conducting (Editions de L'Oiseau-Lyre). The Decca Record Company Limited, London.

In answer to Wittgenstein's despairing conclusion that so little value is achieved by human efforts to find meaning and purpose through philosophy, Bach provides a radical diagnosis of the human condition and need for an external and transcendent, and yet highly personal, answer which are the unique claims of Christianity.

It is our contention that the most important question to answer is that posed by Jesus Christ in the primary source documents that record his life and which we have seen withstand legal scrutiny at every turn. When the apostle Peter, sounding like quite the post-modernist himself, suggested that there were a number of varying interpretations of the nature and character of Jesus floating around Palestine at the time, Jesus asked, "But who do you say that I am?" (Matthew 16:15).

Peter's answer to that question still remains the most evidentially and legally supportable interpretation of the data found in the documents: "You are the Christ, the Son of the living God" (Matthew 16:16).

About the Author

Craig Parton received his Master of Arts in Theology and Law from the Simon Greenleaf School of Law and his Juris Doctorate from the University of California, Hastings College of the Law. He is a trial lawyer and Chairman of the Litigation Department at the oldest law firm in the Western United States, located in Santa Barbara, California, and the former Chairman of the Litigation Section of the Santa Barbara County Bar Association. He is also the United States Director of the International Academy of Apologetics and Human Rights, which meets each year in Strasbourg, France (www.apologeticsacademy.eu). He has contributed numerous articles to cultural, legal, and theological journals. His most recent book is entitled *The Defense Never Rests: A Lawyer among the Theologians* (CPH, 2015).

INDEX